UFOS

 a beginner's guide

TERESA MOOREY

Hodder & Stoughton

A MEMBER OF THE HODDER HEADLINE GROUP

Dedicated to all those who seek the truth.

Acknowledgement

Many thanks to Robin Cole, President of the Circular Forum, for the help he has given me, and for permission to quote extensively from his self-published work 'GCHQ and the UFO Cover-Up'. Please see 'Futher reading' for news and contact number.

Orders: please contact Bookpoint Ltd, 39 Milton Park, Abingdon, Oxon OX14 4TD. Telephone: (44) 01235 827720, Fax: (44) 01235 400454. Lines are open from 9.00–6.00, Monday to Saturday, with a 24 hour message answering service. Email address: orders@bookpoint.co.uk

British Library Cataloguing in Publication Data
A catalogue record for this title is available from The British Library

ISBN 0 340 75834 1

First published 1999
Impression number 10 9 8 7 6 5 4 3 2 1
Year   2005 2004 2003 2002 2001 2000 1999

Typeset by Transet Limited, Coventry, England.
Printed in Great Britain for Hodder & Stoughton Educational, a division of Hodder Headline Plc, 338 Euston Road, London NW1 3BH by Cox and Wyman Limited, Reading, Berks.

CONTENTS

WONDERS IN THE SKY

Man has an innate longing for something he can look up to and admire – for beings who can solve his problems and show him the way to self-improvement.

Colin Wilson, *Starseekers* (Granada, 1982)

The idea of creatures from other worlds has always filled humans with fascination and dread. In 1938 much of the US was flung into panic by Orson Welles on radio, reading with grave conviction from H.G. Well's *The War of the Worlds*, a novel about a Martian invasion. Groups of people fled to the hills, mistaking the broadcast for a genuine news item, and some are even believed to have committed suicide. Speculation about life on Mars has been a twentieth-century preoccupation, starting with astronomer Percival Lowell's 'canals', at the beginning of the century. The belief in these persisted for over 50 years, until the first space probes proved them non-existent. Controversy about the Red Planet continues today, centering on the Cydonia region and the 'Face' which we shall consider later.

Mars may, until fairly recently, have seemed to be the planet most likely to support life. Speculation naturally extends far beyond our solar system, however, to Sirius, the Pleiades and other star systems. The existence of other dimensions and the possibility of travel between them gives the mind plenty of scope to imagine alien craft and visitors strange beyond our dreams. Some people have even suggested that alien craft originate from beneath our oceans, arising

from surviving relics of some lost continent such as Atlantis or Lemuria, preserved underwater by advanced antedeluvian technology. Stories of encounters and abductions abound, and more than a few people believe, chillingly, that aliens are very definitely among us, and that the government is in league with them, offering its citizens for scientific experimentation in return for technological advancement. Some have also suggested that we may share the Earth itself with aliens who live under or within the ground. And here we are in very ancient territory.

Historical encounters of the third kind

Only comparatively recently have we conceived of our world as one among countless globes, hanging in the vastness of space. Theories prior to this placed Earth at the centre of concentric spheres, containing sun, moon and planets. No concept existed of 'other worlds', but there were many ideas about aliens and countless 'abduction' stories. These were described as encounters with gods, demons and fairies, and visits to the Otherworld, a mythological, magical space-time continuum, existing alongside and yet outside our own.

Perhaps the most famous historical 'abduction' was that of Thomas of Ercledoune, known also as 'Thomas the Rhymer'. Thomas lived in Scotland in the thirteenth-century and was widely respected as a prophet and seer – qualities bestowed upon him by the Queen of Elfland, who fell in love with him and abducted him. This could be taken for romantic nonsense, but on closer examination it has several features in common with modern tales of abduction, where sexual experiments are often reported, and mating with strange and beautiful aliens who need our genetic stock to augment their own takes place.

With all accounts, and indeed at all times, as we seek to expand our understanding, I believe we have to remember the limitations

imposed upon us by our conditioning. A story I repeatedly use to illustrate this concerns the landing of the explorer Magellan on the shores of South America. As the Europeans landed in their boats the natives marvelled that they had crossed the vastness of the ocean in such small craft. Laughingly, the travellers pointed at their ocean-going vessels, at anchor out on the waves, but the natives could not see them. Such large ships were totally outside their comprehension, so their brains obligingly censored the messages from their optic nerves. To dismiss this as the limitations of primitive minds is to miss the point. Our brains are undoubtedly 'primitive' by some standards. What else are we missing, *because we do not want to see?*

There are several characteristics that link encounters with so-called 'fairies' and the modern experiences of 'extra-terrestrials'. Firstly, both aliens and fairies seem to like to abduct humans, and these 'abductions' often involve sexual activity and breeding. Traditionally, fairies were said to be attracted to the young, beautiful and talented. Women who had just given birth might be at risk, and so might the baby who could be spirited away, leaving in exchange a 'changeling'. In a society where healthy children were essential for economical survival, the label 'changeling' could provide a tragic excuse for rejecting a child who was sick or deformed. However, these stories tie in with many accounts of how humans have been used for interbreeding, half-alien foetuses taken away to be reunited as fully-formed babies with their human mothers aboard spaceships. Accounts of seductive aliens mating with fortunate human males, in order to 'take their seed' echoes stories of fairy lovers. Of course we know that sexual longing can get mixed up with escapism and yearning for the transcendent. However, sex and procreation are likely to be a preoccupation in any species.

Another common factor concerns cattle. Evil fairies were known to steal cattle, or to drain their life-blood, and it was well known that 'good' fairies loved to receive an offering of milk, from which they would extract the essence, not literally drinking the milk itself. Modern parallels to this are the accounts of weird and macabre 'surgery' carried out on animals, especially cows. Internal organs are removed with a surgical precision unknown to our technology, and the corpse may be drained of blood, with no trace of it spilt. Often

this happens in broad daylight, when the animal has been recently seen alive and well. No traces of footprints or other tracks lead to the animal. Such accounts of inexplicable cattle mutilations date back to the Middle Ages.

The gift of 'prophecy' sometimes conferred upon fairy abductees, such as Thomas the Rhymer, may also be experienced by those taken by aliens. Many people claim to be telepathically in contact with aliens, who tell them about significant future events. One of the most well-known accounts concerns the 'Mothman' prophecies. In the mid 1960s, in Ohio, Kentucky and West Virginia, sighting were reported of a frightening figure, rather like a large human with wings folded at its back and glowing red eyes, apparently able to fly at 100 miles an hour. UFOs were also seen and people of psychic ability began to channel messages from aliens, one of which was an accurate prediction of the death of Robert Kennedy.

'Missing time' is a recurring element in tales of abduction. Those who have had abduction experiences may be unable to account for several hours, and may recover, under hypnosis, memories of meetings with aliens. In addition, whole periods of remembered time have been found to be false, while 'real' memory of multiple abduction is recovered. In traditional fairy encounters time is often also a factor, with Otherworld time passing more swiftly or more slowly than ours. A day spent in the Otherworld may be a year of our time or vice versa.

Signs and wonders

Prior to the 'Age of Reason' any celestial phenomena were explained away as portents from the Divine, as omens and signs. Another explanation for lights in the sky was that they were dragons. Such an observation was recorded in 793, when fiery dragons were seen flying over Northumbria. Similarly in 1113 witnesses saw a celestial beast emerging out of Christchurch Bay, with five fire-breathing heads which set fire to houses and destroyed a ship in the bay. 'Fairy ships' have also been observed, such as that witnessed in

Gravesend, Kent, in 1211, when worshippers coming out of church witnessed a ship in the sky, dangling an 'anchor' which caught on one of the tombstones in the churchyard. A creature from the ship came down towards the anchor, as if swimming in the air, and the congregation, no doubt overcome by Christian zeal, tried to seize him. The bishop told them to stop, and the skyman returned to his vessel, when the anchor was freed and the ship departed. In Medieval France there existed a belief in a land called Magonia, situated beyond the sky and from which ships sailed forth in the clouds. Hapless creatures, believed to be from Magonia, were on show in fairs at the time.

Lights in the sky are as old as humanity, each culture evolving its own explanation in keeping with its beliefs and knowledge. To the ancient Greeks, flying objects would no doubt have been regarded as thunderbolts from Zeus, king of the Olympian deities. The story of Phaethon, son of the Sun god Helios who stole his father's fiery chariot and flew with it so close to the Earth that it was scorched, may in fact be a memory of a UFO visit. In punishment for his violation, Zeus let fly a mighty thunderbolt at the young vandal, killing him outright. Wandering lights were also regarded as the spirits of shamans, in the process of spirit flight to the Otherworld to gather knowledge for the benefit of the tribe, and spiritual revelation. Certain Native Americans still hold such beliefs, while the Chinese believed the gold lights witnessed around sacred peaks, such as Wutaishan, were Bodhisattva lights. A Bodhisattva is one who has attained spiritual perfection, but instead of progressing on to higher realms, elects to stay with humanity, helping others on their evolutionary path.

Closer to the present time was the 1783 sighting of a cigar-shaped object, half the size of the moon, but much brighter. This was witnessed at Windsor Castle in England by some of the scientific elite of the day. Thomas Sandby, a member of the Royal Academy, was among the select group of guests, who saw the apparition on a warm, clear night in August, and he and his brother painted the object, giving a very clear rendition of what he and the others had seen. This was described as an 'oblong cloud' under which could be seen a 'luminous object' which 'became spherical' and from which the light

given off was 'prodigious; it lit up everything on the ground'. It moved off towards the south-east, changing shape as a sort of trail appeared, and seeming to separate into 'two small bodies. Scarcely two minutes later the sound of an explosion was heard'. A fuller account of this is given in *UFOs & Ufology* by Devereux and Brookesmith (see Further reading) and the quotations are from one of the witnesses, Tiberius Cavallo, as given in this work.

The first definable UFO sightings occurred towards the end of the nineteenth century, when 'phantom airships' were spotted in the skies over England and America. They were explained away as being dirigibles (navigable balloons), although at the time of some of the earlier sightings these did not yet exist. In any case, the technical abilities of the unidentified craft were far beyond the scope of anything contemporary. Even before this, however, individuals were claiming to have been 'contacted' by entities from other planets as part of the growing Spiritualist movement. One of the most notable contactees was one Helene Smith, who claimed visions of beings from Mars, in particular one attractive male Martian called Astane, who took her to his home planet to visit. Helene learned how to speak 'Martian' and to write in strange rune-like symbols. With the help of professor Flournoy from Geneva University, who was making a psychological study of her, these experiences were brought together in a book called *From India to the Planet Mars*.

Born in 1874, the journalist and philosopher Charles Fort is one of the best-known names in the realm of paranormal investigation, even giving his name to all such as 'Fortean' phenomena. A great wit and sceptic, Fort observed how often so-called objective scientists distort facts to make them fit their own or other accepted theories. Fort catalogued a large number of anomalies and oddities in his works *The Book of the Damned*, *Lo!*, *New Lands* and *Wild Talents*, including the raining of strange objects such as frogs, people and beasts that mysteriously appear and disappear and, of course, lights in the sky. From the mass of data accumulated, Fort developed the belief that there really did exist a race of extra-terrestrials, who had been in contact with selected humans for some time. He even entertained the possibility that these beings might pose a threat.

In the years leading up to World War I, lights in the sky and large objects were seen in the skies over Britain, France, the Netherlands and Germany. There were worries that the Germans possessed some advanced technology, but they too were puzzled by the sightings. The manoeuverability of the craft and the speeds witnessed far exceeded anything possible at that time. Intriguing 'encounters' were also reported, for instance the appearance of beings about 4ft (1¼m) tall near a cigar-shaped landed craft, in Hamburg in the summer of 1914.

Between the two World Wars there were countless 'sightings'. In Scandinavia in the 1930s grey flying machines were often spotted in conditions of bad weather, circling low over the ground and scanning with searchlights. Two Swedish aircraft were lost trying to discover the nature of these craft. Prior to this in 1992 a 'plane' had been seen to fall amazingly slowly into the sea near Barmouth, Wales, but no aircraft were reported missing and no wreckage was found. In 1927 a cigar-shaped object was seen to emerge from behind a cloud over San Francisco Bay. The cigar-shaped mother ship from which smaller 'saucers' emerge has become part of UFO lore. The above are just a few selected incidents from a vast body of evidence.

The weaving of the saucery

The beginning of the use of the term 'flying saucer' dates back to 24 June 1947, when an Idaho pilot named Kenneth Arnold reported seeing nine bright objects flying at unbelievable velocity. Arnold was employed by the US Forest Service and was out on a search for a missing aircraft. He spotted the 'saucers' at 3 p.m., between Mount Ranier and Mount Adams in Washington State. They appeared to be weaving in and out of formation, at a speed that Arnold estimated must be 1,200 mph (2,000 kmph). His story was supported by a man from Utah, who had reported the sightings of similar objects flying near Ukiah the day before. The interest of the public and the press was intense, but mockery followed and Arnold stated at a later date that he regretted ever having mentioned seeing the 'saucers'.

However, Arnold's report was to be just the beginning, and similar reports began to come in from all over the country. At first the press were interested, but this declined as the stories became increasingly bizarre and far-fetched. Across the world, saucer-shaped craft has also been reported in Christchurch, New Zealand, with a nurse claiming to have seen a flying object like an upturned saucer. The craft had windows, through which she claimed to have seen humanoid shapes. Before this sighting, as far back as 1878, a Texan farmer had seen something travelling at great speed that looked like a saucer. Similar sightings were recorded in the few weeks prior to Arnold's own encounter. Arnold himself never used the term 'flying saucer', but described the craft as shaped like tadpoles or boomerangs, with erratic movements like a saucer might make if you skipped it over water. However, the press machine churned out the term 'saucer-like' and it embedded itself deeply into the popular imagination. A fact which may in itself be significant, as we shall examine in a later chapter.

In many ways the time was ripe for new myths. Science dismissed dragons, sidelined the Divine and regarded spirit flight and shamanism as primitive superstition. However, science encouraged its own mythology. The US had emerged from World War II technologically and economically powerful, while Europe and Russia struggled to rebuild themselves. Space travel was on the horizon and science fiction foreshadowed this. (Science fiction is very often the precursor to science fact, with visionary scientists building on the works of sci-fi authors.) In addition, a growing element of paranoia existed in a battle-scarred world. No-one in the West quite knew just how advanced the Russians were. In such a hot-house climate stories about secret weapons and experiments, cover-ups, misinformation and disinformation could grow, luxuriantly, along with beliefs in theories of government conspiracy, the cynical trade-off to aliens of citizens for experimentation in return for technology, mind-control and – well, almost anything, for the sky wasn't, and isn't the limit. But here we run ahead of ourselves.

MORE SIGHTINGS

Over the last 50 years, thousands and thousands of unexplained flying objects have been seen and many credible witnesses, such as aircraft pilots and military personnel, have gone on record as saying they have seen something, and that they feel it cannot be explained by any known means or technology. Countless photographs and video footage are also available. Naturally many videos of unidentified craft are indistinct and 'wobbly', and so are laid wide open to accusation of being fake, or mistake. However, Robin Cole of the Circular Forum (see Resources) makes the following highly valid point:

> You imagine what it is like suddenly to spot something in the sky and to realise that it is a UFO. How would you feel? What would you do? Is it not likely that you would be very agitated, very excited? You would be doing quite well to find your camcorder at all, let alone switch it on and work it. At the same moment you're jumping up and down yelling at your family to come and see the thing, you're trying to track it and video it. The wonder is that there are so many reasonable videos of these objects at all, and it is hardly surprising that the picture isn't always well-focused or steady.

In fact there are many videos of UFOs, so many that it is hard to maintain doubt that something is going on. Perhaps it has always been 'going on', but in the latter half of the twentieth century it has been increasingly successfully documented.

In the 1950s one George Adamski took a number of photographs in the grounds of the observatory on Mount Palomar, California. These showed classic shapes such as the saucers and cigar-shaped mother ships in great detail. Adamski said he had encountered an alien in the desert, tall, with green eyes and long blond hair, and this creature had taken him to Venus, Mars and Saturn. The aliens said they were making contact with Earth at this crucial time because of the threat presented by nuclear weapons, which were a danger not only to us but to other life forms. However, the authenticity of Adamski's photographs was regarded as questionable. When it

emerged that 'professor' Adamski did not work at the observatory itself but in a café, his credibility went steeply downhill, although interest in his accounts remained.

UFO sightings are known to occur in waves, with clusters of many sightings in a particular location, followed by a relative lull. Some years ago sightings in the Cotswolds, England, were a regularity, but for the last couple of years all has remained relatively quiet. Certain locations are also favoured over others, and some readers will remember that Warminster, for instance, was the UFO capital of Britain in the 1960s and 1970s. Sightings seem to be more common where other paranormal activity is also encountered, leading to the formulation of the theory that UFOs are from some other order of reality, to which access is more readily gained at certain locations where certain 'energies' in the earth are high. However, this theory does not account for many of the reported encounters with strange craft and their occupants.

Encounters with Greys

On 11 October 1973 one of the most famous and dramatic UFO encounters took place. Two shipyard workers, Calvin Parker and Charles Hickson, were fishing in the Pascagoula River, Mississippi. About two miles (3¼km) away they spotted a weird blue light which swooped towards them until it was only about 40ft (12m) away. An oblong shape was revealed within the light, hovering about 10ft (3m) over the water. The men heard a buzz, an opening formed in the oblong shape and three creatures came floating towards them, took hold of them and carried them into the 'ship'. The younger man, Parker, who was only 18, passed out from fright but Hickson remained conscious. In common with many people Hickson describes 'Greys', creatures with silvery skin with slits for eyes and no hair, pointy ears and claw-like hands. Hickson was examined by a big eye-like contraption, while he was hanging horizontally in midair in a brightly lit room.

The two were then returned to the bank of the river, where the younger man recovered consciousness. However, their ordeal was far from over for they were besieged by reporters, doubters determined to make them a laughing stock and the equally disconcerting contingent of fanatics who wanted to canonize them. The men displayed no evidence at all of drinking, and were visibly upset. The tough, 45-year-old Hickson broke down into tears and the teenager was heard to pray. Hickson asked to take a lie-detector test, which he passed. No-one else saw the event itself, but there were other similar reports of UFO sightings in the area on the days around the major event. Not surprisingly the abduction haunted Hickson, who kept thinking about getting in touch with the aliens. Lots of scepticism greeted the entire episode. The writer Philip Klass, an arch UFO debunker, regards the episode as a hoax, questioning the good character of Charles Hickson and the qualifications of the polygraphist who tested him (Philip Klass, *UFOs Explained*, New York Random House, 1974). Other researchers have classified this encounter as hallucination. On the other hand, the local sheriff believed that something had indeed happened, because the two men were so scared he believed they were close to heart attack.

As always, in such incidents, you can take your choice about who or what to believe. I am sure that any of us, excitedly describing something amazing that had happened to us, might change details as we calmed down, more clearly evaluated and chose our words. Certain variable details in Hickson's account may not, with this in mind, be so suspicious. And most of us, too, have something discreditable in our past that any character-assassin might seize upon, as some did with Hickson's earlier sacking from a supervisor's job. Similarly, those who wish to believe will always, where necessary, find a way round the facts.

Coming back across the globe to Devon, England, on the night of 24 October 1967, two policemen chased a huge, luminous flying cross for a distance of 12 miles (20km). This subsequently disappeared, but was spotted in other areas of the country. A spokesman from the MOD said that what the witnesses had seen were two American planes refuelling, an explanation which was refuted by the American Air Command.

Two days after this on the downs in Dorset, retired flight Administrative Officer and RAF photographic interpreter Angus Brooks was walking his dogs. Pounded by a fierce wind, he decided to lie down for a while in the shelter of a hollow, when he saw an object shooting out of the sky, towards the ground. The object stopped at about 250ft (75m) above the ground. It had a central disk about 25ft (7½m) across and 12ft (3½m) in depth, and four protruding fusilages, about three times the craft's diameter, which formed a cross. When it stopped descending it rotated through 90 degrees clockwise and silently hovered, completely unaffected by the wind. It appeared to be made of something translucent that took on the colour of the sky. Despite the attempts of his German shepherd dog to drag him away, Brooks remained, watching the thing for 20 minutes, when it finally took off towards the north-east. Subsequent walks to the area made the dog very nervous and she died six weeks later of acute cystitis.

Brooks had undergone a corneal transplant some years before and an MOD investigator decided that the UFO was just a piece of loose matter floating in his eyeball. Combined with the recent UFO publicity and a dreamy state resulting from his rest, this had induced the UFO vision. Not surprisingly, Brooks denied this, pointing out that pieces of matter in the eye would move with the eye, and this had quite clearly behaved very differently.

Flying crosses are one class of UFO, which are commonly reported and described. These also have their place in history, and it is not surprising that objects in the sky in the shape of a cross should have been regarded with dread by medieval Christians. In April 1561, in Nüremberg, southern Germany, red, black and blue objects of various shapes were seen in the sky, some of them in the form of crosses. Those watching not surprisingly believed they were witness to some celestial battle, and some of the objects fell to earth in an emission of vapour.

Reports of UFOs have been documented throughout history. The strange coloured objects seen in Nuremberg in 1561 were recorded in the local broadsheet.

fatima

The sightings at Fatima, Portugal on 13 May 1917, are not regarded by everyone as UFO encounters, but rather as a religious experience. In this incident ten-year-old Lucia dos Santos and her two cousins saw wonders in the sky and a lady in a white robe. This happened again each month until October. After the first sightings, crowds came in ever-growing numbers, to watch what happened. There would be a flash of light and the sunlight would seem to grow less powerful. A shining sphere, sometimes apparently 'buzzing', stationed itself over a tree, accompanied sometimes by a white cloud, and on two occasions something described as 'angel's hair' floated to earth. Thousands saw the globe but only the three original witnesses were able to see the woman at the centre.

On 13 October the huge crowd that had gathered to watch had a dreadful fright. All appeared to be over, and the rain was pouring down, when the clouds miraculously parted to reveal a brilliant globe, spinning in the sky. When the globe stilled its motion and began to fall towards the earth, all assembled fell to their knees and prayed, fearing it was the sun falling from the sky. But the object never reached the ground. Instead it flew into the sun and disappeared, leaving the ground and the sodden clothes of the worshippers completely dry.

A shrine has been built at Fatima and it is now a place of pilgrimage for Catholics. However, many people believe this was not a religious vision but a UFO encounter. No-one but Lucia could hear the words of the sky-lady, and some have put this down to telepathy between her and the 'alien'. Predictions were made to Lucia and many of them have come true. One contained a secret prophecy, for the eyes of the papacy alone. Pope John XXIII opened this in 1960, but the contents were never revealed. Lucia became a nun and her cousins died not long after the encounter.

Cults and contactees

The Fatima sighting has been embraced by the established Church as a form of contact with the Divine. However, it is more usual for people who claim to have been in contact with extra-terrestrials to inaugurate or to find themselves at the head of a new cult. Although based on a literal belief in extra-terrestrial life, the message is essentially a spiritual one, of benign beings watching over the earth in turbulent times, of a united universe and of spiritual revelation available to humankind through the medium of the extra-terrestrials and their contacts. This is all part of the New Age, where spirituality is no longer the sole province of the Church, and where people are free to develop their individual approach. The New Age embraces many concepts and movements, not all of them enlightened, or even 'sensible', but the faith in and desire for a new era of peace and wisdom is at least encouraging. To many contactees, revelation will come from the 'space people' and the Second Coming will take the

form of a mass landing of advanced aliens, who will assist the earth in a move towards higher knowledge.

Much of the information from the space beings come through 'channelling', a modern form of mediumship. The channeller simply allows words and pictures to be sent through them, some going into a fairly deep trance, while others just seem to hear voices, inaudible to others. Channelled messages of all sorts are very fashionable, and they do not only come from extra-terrestrials, but from many different sources, such as spirit guides of Native American lineage, ancient Egyptians and others. While much of this is at best plain silly, and at worst a life-wrecking illusion, there is no doubt that channelling is a powerful tool for accessing a fund of knowledge not normally available to the conscious mind. This takes us into territory outside everyday reality and our normal terms of reference. Aliens and deceased Tibetans may be simply the personas with which our conscious mind clothes the source of our information. Be that as it may, many people insist that they are literally in contact with people from other worlds, through telepathy and channelling.

One of the most notable of these was George King, an erstwhile London taxi driver. In 1954, at the age of 34, King heard a voice telling him to prepare himself to become the voice of the Interplanetary Parliament. George King was already involved with yoga and Eastern spiritual philosophy and the message did not break his stride. With the aid of an Indian yogi he made contact with a Venusian named Aetherius, who gave him many messages. These he published in a news letter, and so acquired a following, as a result of which The Aetherius Society was founded in 1956. King has received various accolades and was a governor of the Royal National Lifeboat Institution in England.

The Aetherius Society has branches worldwide and still flourishes. It works by attempting to influence global events through the power of prayer. King has written several books, among which is *You Are Responsible!* (1961) and in which he describes his out-of-body experiences on Mars, and his defeat of a malevolent meteor with earth's name on it through the pure power of love. The Aetherius Society believes that life exists on many levels of vibration and dimensions, hence the inexplicable disappearance of many UFOs.

Interdimensional travel is possible through very advanced technology that utilizes the power of thought.

Another contactee, Eduard 'Billy' Meier, first encountered aliens in January 1975, near his home at Hinwel, Zurich, when a disc-shaped silver craft 25ft (7½m) wide landed some way ahead of him. Over the following two hours Billy Meier made the acquaintance of a visitor from the Pleiades star system. This was only the beginning, for over the next 25 years Meier had regular contact with several Pleiadians. These beings looked like earthly Scandinavians, and the females were very beautiful. Meier took more than 1000 relevant photographs, made extensive notes of the sayings of the extra-terrestrials and supposedly collected Pleiadian artefacts. Meier described the Pleiadians as far advanced compared to earthlings with a life span of 1000 years. These beings had originated in a system in the constellation Lyra and had emigrated to the Pleiades millions of years earlier. Their ships travelled through hyperspace, and time-travel was obviously no problem for them, for they took Meier with them back to prehistory, where he photographed dinosaurs and cavemen.

For a contactee Meier's behaviour is unusual, in that he has produced 'evidence' where as George King and others have relied in their telepathic testimony. Meier's photographs are regarded as fakes by experts and the alien samples are not believed to be genuine. However, this has not deterred the true believers who form his coterie, some of whom are alleged to have made threats against those who wish to defame him, hinting at conspiracy and victimization.

Not all of those who believe in alien contact regard it as by any means benevolent, for there are those who claim that the aliens are devils in disguise, good old-fashioned Satan, come to wreak havoc and misery upon humankind. Sadly, this approach has found favour with more established ufologists than any salvationist beliefs, perhaps because it falls more in line with fundamentalist monotheistic dogmas. Such dogmas hold that only sanctioned texts, such as the Bible are true, and thus anything that might create alternative scenarios for existence must be the work of Satan.

Devereux and Brookesmith (see Further reading) make the following important points:

[The UFO cults] are no more irrational than any other religion, if rashly prone to garble the vocabulary of modern science and put it through an occult mangle to serve their various cosmologies. But they do demonstrate the ready capacity of ufological beliefs to act as fertile soil for religious beliefs...

SOME IMPLICATIONS

When we enter the realms of ufology, we are not merely sifting facts, evaluating evidence. The question inevitably expands, from whether there is really intelligent life on other planets, and whether it has found its way to our own world, to far greater issues that involve our place in the universe, our future, and even the nature of reality itself. If there are beings from other worlds, humanity is faced with an identity crisis. The possibility of panic cannot be ruled out, and that may be one rather poor excuse for the apparent cover-ups. Another possibility is that the presence of alien life could serve to unite humanity, creating a cosmic perspective – this is the attractive scenario portrayed in the Star Trek film *First Contact*, where Vulcans, realizing from the appearance of a warp signature in the solar system that humans have acquired warp drive, land in North America, and so begins a total revolution in the outlook of our species.

Is it too cynical to suggest that perhaps that event might be less than welcome in some quarters? In *The Mars Mystery* (see Further reading) Hancock *et al.* make some important points concerning the possibility of an asteroid colliding with the earth in the coming century. They observe that despite the fact that we have the technology to detect such an object while still far out in space (as displayed by IRAS, the Infrared Astronomical Satellite, launches in January 1983 and going out of action in November that year) the amounts we invest in such a programme are paltry. Only by pooling our technological expertise at the highest international level could we hope to destroy such an object before it blew us into oblivion (as the K/T asteroid is believed to have done to the dinosaurs). Far, far larger amounts of money and energy are invested in fabricating more sophisticated ways of destroying each other, and those in power are

occupied with increasing that power or holding on to it. On a smaller scale, the great majority of us are preoccupied with our own petty striving, that can be harmful and malicious, and are at best trivial in the larger scheme of things. No 'conspiracy' is needed, merely a subconscious collective myopia. The bottom line is that we don't want to open our eyes. Despite the warnings of eminent scientists such as Sir Fred Hoyle, we do not want to believe we may be struck by an asteroid, because it would be too distracting from the business of our lives. By the same token, perhaps we are reluctant to believe in the existence of extra-terrestrials. It is too unsettling. It threatens to underline the establishment in more ways than one.

Science is supposed to be impartial, and yet studies show that statistics, for instance, tend mysteriously to swing towards the bias of the person collecting them. History also shows that more than one eminent scientist has defended beliefs well beyond their sell-by date, because their ego and their reputation have depended upon them. Seeing is believing, believing is seeing. So what is a poor boy (or girl) to do? Hold on to your common sense, and keep your eyes – and your mind – open.

PRACTICE

At this point you may like to review your theories and beliefs about UFOs and extra-terrestrials. Do you believe in them, do you disbelieve, or do you remain to be convinced? And why do you believe what you believe? Do you have a vested interest? For instance, if you are something of an idol-smasher, you may like the thought of powerful scientists and government officials being made to look like kids sucking gobstoppers by some ineffable, 1000-year-old prophet from Sirius. Or if, for some reason, you have lots invested in the status quo, you may prefer to brush all such notions aside. Perhaps knowledge of the cosmos has to start with a little self-knowledge, or at least self-questioning.

If you would like more information you might start by contacting some of the groups and periodicals listed at the back of the book. True scepticism is a healthy state – it is the state of the impartial, open mind, not the professional de-bunker.

The Roswell Incident

The truth is rarely pure and never simple. Modern life would be very tedious if it were either, and modern literature a complete impossibility

The Importance of Being Earnest, Oscar Wilde, 1895

The Roswell story

The table of the crashed saucer at Roswell holds pride of place in UFO lore. Over a half-century has passed since the 'crash' and still there is debate about whether anything really took place or whether the entire incident is a mixture of poor memory and fabrication on the part of those involved. This is how the story goes.

In July 1947, near Roswell, New Mexico, a spaceship crashed in the desert. The American Air Force issued a press release to the effect that it had captured a flying saucer, but this was speedily retracted and instead they said they had recovered a crashed weather balloon. Witnesses and the local radio station were quickly silenced with various attendant threats on the part of the authorities. There may have been two 'crash sites', one where debris from an in-flight explosion was scattered, and another where the craft itself, complete with occupants, hit the ground. Reports circulated about several recovered humanoid corpses upon whom autopsies were performed.

The debris apparently included indestructible, but very light, material resembling plastic, some strange metallic substance that could be bent all ways but retained its original shape, and some mysterious hieroglyphics that looked Egyptian or Chinese written on a lilac-pink material. The remains were taken to Roswell Base, home of the elite 509th Squadron, repository for America's nuclear capability. From there they were flown to Wright-Paterson Base under conditions of tight security. Since then the authorities have persistently denied that anything at all significant ever took place at Roswell. No ultimate proof has been produced, either to support the belief that a saucer, complete with aliens, did in fact crash in the desert, or to discredit completely several key witnesses. Let us look at the story from the perspective of these witnesses.

Major Jesse Marcel

Jesse Marcel was Intelligence Officer at the Roswell Base. He had been flying since 1928 and described himself as being familiar with almost everything that flew. A skilled cartographer, he was sent to intelligence school by the Army Air Force, following the attack on Pearl Harbour, and was soon promoted to instructor. On combat duty he later went to New Guinea where he became Intelligence Officer for his bomber squadron and later for the whole group. He logged 468 hours of combat flying in B-24s and was awarded five medals for shooting down enemy aircraft. Near the end of the war he was chosen to become part of the 509th bomb wing of the American Army Air Force. All members of this were carefully selected, as it was the only atomic bomb group in the world at the time, and everyone involved had to have security clearance at the highest level.

Marcel said that the wreckage he saw was scattered over an area of about ¾ mile long (1.2 kilometres) and several hundred yards wide. The Roswell Base heard about the crash when they received a telephone call from the Roswell county sheriff, saying that a certain Mac Brazell had reported that something had exploded over his ranch. Marcel drove out to investigate, driving over very rough

country in his Buick. According to Marcel, the wreckage he saw was definitely not that of a weather balloon, but something he had never seen before, or since. He and his companion gathered the fragments, which consisted of small pieces of a material that looked like balsa wood and weighed about the same, but were very hard, despite their flexibility, and would not burn. On these fragments were inscribed hieroglyphics. They also recovered a quantity of a strong parchment-like substance and fragments of what looked like tinfoil, but wasn't. One of his colleagues found a light-weight black metallic box, a few inches square. Of all the bits and pieces recovered the 'tinfoil' was the most interesting, because although it would flex back and forth it was impossible to crease it. It could not be torn or cut and a 16-lb (7-kg) sledgehammer failed to dent it. The best description Marcel could make of this substance was that it was like a metal with plastic properties.

All the debris that could be loaded up was taken back to the base where salvagers found that stories of a crashed flying disc had preceded them. The Public Information Officer on the base had given out the story, and Marcel heard that he was later severely reprimanded by his superiors for giving out the press release, although he did not know that for sure. The next day, under orders from the colonel, the entire wreckage was flown by Marcel to Carswell, Fort Worth, where the general took control and organized someone else to fly the stuff to Wright Patterson Field, for analysis. Marcel was told not to talk to the press under any circumstances. Some of the wreckage was taken to the general's office at Carswell and photographed by the press, along with Marcel holding some of the less remarkable remnants. No-one was allowed close enough to touch the material. Marcel states that later photographs were taken while all the true wreckage was en route to Wright Patterson, and was of some substituted materials.

Marcel believes that General Ramey concocted the balloon cover story to keep the press quiet. The press were also told that the Wright-Patterson flight was cancelled when it was not. Marcel, however, was taken off that flight and someone else took the controversial wreckage on the final stage of its journey. Marcel could tell the press nothing because he was under orders. The press simply did not see

the most interesting parts, including the hieroglypics, and they were told that what had been recovered was simply a weather balloon. Marcel kept silence, as ordered, and was transferred to Washington DC three months later, where he was promoted to the rank of Lieutenant Colonel as part of a special weapons programme, collecting air samples from all over the world to ascertain whether or not the Soviets had exploded their first atomic bomb. When President Truman went on the air with a statement that the Russians had indeed exploded such a device, he was reading from Marcel's report.

Marcel's son remembers that his father was gone for a couple of days at the time in question, and returned with a vehicle full of debris. He recalls shredded black plastic that looked organic and pieces of thin, tough metal, with some beams. His father told him that these things were classified, and so he was not to take any of it. Dr Marcel (junior) has since deeply regretted this. His impression was that the debris was from some machine and not a weather balloon. His father had said that the speed of the impact was not in keeping with any contemporary aircraft. On the edges of the beams that he saw, Dr Marcel (junior) recalls there were purplish pink inscriptions like hieroglyphics. The debris was spread out on their kitchen floor but there was far too much of it to reconstruct. Some of the debris was in fact left behind on the desert ground but it seems that subsequently the area was examined with a fine tooth comb by Air Force Intelligence and anything remaining would no doubt have been reclaimed.

Marcel's evidence provides in many ways the foundation of the case for the crashed saucer. However, his detractors assert that his official service record does not bear out his claims concerning his war record. His combat flying was limited to the job of passenger as an intelligence observer and he was awarded two medals simply for flying the necessary number of missions. He had no arms ability, no degree and no knowledge of weather balloons or radar tracking equipment. His promotion to Lieutenant Colonel was never an active service rank but in the reserve. He was not shot down in combat (as he claims) and there is no evidence that he was involved, however remotely, in the announcement by President Truman concerning Russian nuclear tests, which in any case was not made on the radio.

Further than this, it is a mistake to assume that military personnel should have no problem recognizing a weather balloon, because at the time most did not know anything about them. Marcel is described as giving an inflated impression of most parts of his life and of having a slender connection with reality.

Marcel's testimony is among the most important in the annals of Roswell. If he was not telling the truth, then the case for the crashed saucer is severely dented. However, it is a sad and rather alarming comment on the elite US 509th Bomber Group, custodians of the most destructive weapon known on earth, that they employed as their intelligence officer a Walter Mitty fantasist. Of course it is also an alarming thought that the US military could have deliberately concealed from the American public and the world all evidence of extra-terrestrials and their wrecked craft.

Mac Brazel

'Mac' was the nickname for William Brazel, the rancher who allegedly discovered pieces of strange wreckage on his land. He died in 1963, so his story comes through his son and daughter-in-law, and others who knew him. However, it is not possible to ascertain everything that happened, because Mac Brazel was very reluctant to speak of it, and information is therefore sketchy. According to his relatives, the military swore him to secrecy and he would not even speak of his experience to his wife.

His son and daughter-in-law first heard of the Roswell business when they saw Mac's picture on the front of the local paper, the *Albuquerque Journal*. According to this, Mac had heard something explode over his ranch and had found debris strewn all around, and so had gone to the local sheriff to report what had happened. It should be noted that, at the time leading up to the incident, there had been many sightings of unidentified 'craft' especially near sensitive military bases in the US, and on the night in question there were exceptional thunderstorms raging. Mac described these as the worst he'd ever seen and noticed that the lightning was being

attracted again and again to the same spots. It was in the middle of a storm that he had heard a noise not consistent with normal thunder. However, he had thought little more about it until he found the wreckage, and this did not apparently impress him unduly until he went into town on Saturday 5 July where he heard many stories about flying saucers that had been spotted locally. On Sunday 6 July he thought seriously about what had come down on his ranch and decided he had better do something about it, hence his report to the sheriff. This gave rise to the newspaper publicity and a press release by the base to the effect that a flying saucer had been captured, and the beginnings of the entire matter we now know as the Roswell Incident.

Naturally concerned about him, his relatives went to the ranch to find him absent. By 14 July, when Mac had still not returned, his son began to make enquiries. He received assurances that he was all right and that he would be home soon, which proved to be correct. However, on his return Mac was very terse about the whole matter and would say no more about what he had found. What he did say was that if he ever found anything else they would have a hard time getting him to say anything at all about it, unless it was a bomb! He had been shut away, and was indignant and puzzled that for doing what he saw as a dutiful deed he had been put in jail, and given a full head-to-toe physical examination by the army doctor before they would release him. They had sworn him to secrecy as a patriotic trust, but the event had left him discouraged and disillusioned. However, there are details which 'flesh out' the account of the wreckage.

The debris was scattered over a length of about a quarter of a mile, and it seemed obvious that whatever it had come from had blown up. Mac felt that it was obvious that the craft had been flying along the airline path, to Socorro. It is easy to imagine that a 'straight dirt' rancher, out checking on his sleep, might not feel that the wreckage was very important. His trip to town changed that, and he went back for a closer look. His son also saw much of the wreckage, and in fact collected quite a portion of it, for more would come to the surface after each hard rain. He described pieces of a wood-like substance, that was very hard and quite unbreakable, and a type of tinfoil that wouldn't tear or wrinkle. Mac told his son that the army had

established that it was not anything made contemporarily in the US. In addition there was a thread-like material, or possibly wire, that would not break. Mac had also seen markings like hieroglyphics on bits that he found. Mac's son boasted about his collection of strange materials one night, about two years after the incident, while on an evening out. The next day he had a visit from a captain at the Roswell Base who asked to see the materials. Describing it as most important to the security of the country, he took the collection away with him. He also asked to be taken to the spot where the debris had been found, where he and others looked for any other remnants. Finding none, he told Brazel junior to contact him if he ever found any more pieces. However, none were found.

Mac had seen plenty of downed weather balloons, and said that this was no such thing. Nor did he find anything resembling an instrument package. Another detail noticed by Mac was that some of the vegetation in the vicinity of the crash was singed at the tips. Interestingly, when Brazel junior was working in Alaska, he was talking to a man about a flying saucer that was supposed to have landed in that part of the world and, naturally, the topic of Mac's find came up. The person he was talking to appeared to have more information than he did, saying that further wreckage and been found in the desert, and along with it the bodies of some dead and dying creatures, about 4ft (1¼m) in height. This suggests that there may have been more than one crash site involved in the 'incident'.

Floyd Proctor, Mac's closest neighbour, described how excited the rancher had been about this find, saying it was the oddest stuff he'd ever seen, how it resembled paper but could not be cut, and that it had Chinese or Japanese designs on parts of it. Proctor and another neighbour had seen Mac during his 'detention' period in Roswell, surrounded by military personnel, and he had walked straight past his friends without any acknowledgement. Proctor's brother-in-law was involved in flying the wreckage to Fort Worth, who had asked others on the flight whether what they were transporting was really the remains of a flying saucer. He was told that it was and that he mustn't ask any more questions.

Mac's younger son and daughter were with him when the wreckage was originally found. His daughter apparently denied all possibility

of debris being anything like a weather balloon, because they had seen many of them. She was particularly taken with the columns of strange figures which she took to be some sort of numbering, although they resembled nothing she had ever seen. She remembers being told by the military to keep quiet about the entire matter. Whatever the debris were, one thing is certain – the military were undoubtedly very interested in it indeed, for all the wreckage was carefully scraped up and the area virtually sieved.

The owner of KGFL Radio, W.E. Whitmore, apparently interviewed Mac at the time of the find and planned to broadcast the dialogue as a 'scoop'. He hid Mac at his home to maintain exclusivity, at a time when the military were searching for him. Whitmore began broadcasting a preliminary release locally when a call came through from the Secretary of the Federal Communications Commission in Washington DC, who told him in no uncertain terms that the matter involved national security and if he didn't keep quiet about it he would lose his licence. This was backed up by a call from Senator Chavez of New Mexico. The broadcast was never made. Whitmore also saw some of the wreckage and his descriptions tally with those of Mac.

So it seems that Mac Brazel may have discovered wreckage from some interplanetary craft that had begun to distinegrate, and was due to crash further out in the desert. In fact, another site is reported to have been involved, at San Augustin, but this would have been the province of the air base at Alamogordo. Security here was even tighter than at Roswell, because of the tests that were being carried out on V2 type rockets and the military would no doubt have swooped upon anything controversial. We must not forget that far from alien threats, the preoccupation of the US forces at that time centred upon Russian military capability, as the Cold War was under way. And that brings us to a more likely possibility. The wreckage that caused all the excitement could have been the remains of a top secret experiment on the part of the Americans, or, for that matter, the Russians. Whatever it was, preserving its secrecy was of the utmost importance to the military.

The undertaker's testimony

Glenn Dennis was 22 in 1947, and was assistant at Ballard's Funeral Home, the Roswell undertakers, who had a close working relationship with the base. Having only graduated from the San Francisco Mortuary College the summer previously, at the time of the Roswell incident Dennis was little more than a general dogs-body for his firm, although he later rose to the position of Chairman at the New Mexico State Board of Funeral Directors and Embalmers. In July 1947 he received a telephone call from the mortuary officer at Roswell who asked him a 'hypothetical' question: did they have any 3 to 4ft (1 to 1¼m) long hermetically sealed caskets? The funeral home had one. How long would it take to get more, he was asked, 'just for information'. Dennis replied that they could be there the following morning, and asked if there had been a crash. This was denied. Later he was asked several more questions by the same person: how would one handle bodies that had been in the desert for several days? What was embalming fluid made of? What effect did it have on human tissue? Is it possible to seal wounds made by predators? What is the best way to collect such remains? Dennis gave all the information, no doubt glad to be asked for his newly acquired knowledge. Again, any questions he asked about a crash were denied.

Ballard's Funeral Home was also contracted to run an ambulance service for the base, and as it happened, an hour after the final phone call Dennis was instructed to take an injured airman back to the base. The guard at the security barrier recognized Dennis and the injured airman (who was sitting, nursing a wounded hand, in the front of the hearse) and the vehicle was waved through. This was only to be expected. Dennis and the hearse were a frequent sight at the base, and in addition Dennis was an honorary member of the Officer's Club. The undertaker's apprentice drove over to the hospital area and reversed into his usual parking space, pulling up alongside two field ambulances which were guarded by a military policeman.

Naturally curious, Dennis peeped inside and spotted a quantity of thin, metallic material, two curved pieces of metal and some strange markings, like hieroglyphs. Dennis continued into the hospital building, and remarked to an unknown officer that it seemed they had a crash and should he go and prepare his equipment at the funeral home?

What happened next took the undertaker completely by surprise, the more so because he was used to enjoying very friendly, relaxed relations with everyone at the base. The unfamiliar officer asked him who the hell he was and ordered him off the base, but when the young man complied he was hauled back by two military police to receive a barrage of threats. Dennis was outraged and quoted his citizen's rights, whereupon, it is reported, a threat was made against his life, should he speak of what happened to anyone (not, of course, that anything *had* happened, at this point!).

Two military police were called to escort Dennis back to the funeral home, but as they were going down the corridor a door opened and a distressed nurse appeared with a towel over her face. Dennis recognized her as part of the staff at the base and they both stopped in surprise. Two men came out of the same room, behind the nurse, also holding towels to their faces, and Glenn Dennis glimpsed behind them some of the wheeled beds used to ferry patients to and from the operating theatre. Needless to say, with the two military policemen at his elbows, Dennis couldn't examine any further. However, the nurse phoned him the next day and arranged to meet him at the Officer's Club.

At that meeting the nurse related how a flying saucer had crashed in the desert and that three corpses had been salvaged. These were apparently of extra-terrestrials, two of whom were in very bad condition, but the third was fairly intact. These were somewhat smaller than adult human beings. They had four fingers ending in suction pads on each hand, instead of five, and no thumbs. The structure of the arm was different from a human's, with a shortened bone from the shoulder to the elbow. Their heads were large and all the features, including the large eyes, were concave. She drew a sketch for him, which has seemingly been lost. She further told

Dennis that the two men who had come out of the room behind her were pathologists from Washington DC. The towels over their faces were to fend off the terrible stench, and they had come out of the room for some relief from it, because they were wretching.

Dennis promised not to tell anyone what his friend had revealed. She was obviously very upset and had started to cry, so Dennis thought it best to take her back to her quarters in the base. This was to be the last time he saw her. He heard she had been transferred to England, and obtained an address to write to her, only to have his letters returned marked 'Addressee Deceased'. He was later told that she had been killed in a plane crash.

Elements in the story of Dennis seem doubtful. For instance, why would the unknown officer threaten him in such a sinister and violent way? Is it not more probable that appeals would have been made to his patriotism and the matter conducted more subtly? And yet we have the account of the detention of Mac Brazel to support the theory that the military were hiding something. Some people in power like frightening others, especially the ignorant and vulnerable, which is what the young undertaker was. Another point, the doctors emerged from the room where the 'alien' corpses lay without protective clothing – an unlikely scenario, bearing in mind the possibility of contamination. Some researchers appear to have the 'name' of the nurse and assert that no such person ever existed, as proven by records of the time. Tim Shawcross (see Further reading) states that Dennis never revealed her name and describes the undertaker as follows:

> '...an elderly, grey-haired man of ascetic appearance, tall and in good health. Like several of the other eyewitnesses of aspects of the incident, he is a sober and respectable individual about whom many members of the community speak highly. He tends to become somewhat irascible when he finds himself pestered by journalists and tourists, and this reluctance to repeat his story to all and sundry ... counts in his favour ... he has no discernable motive for creating such a wild fantasy out of which he could, if he wished, make money.'

Lieutenant Walter Haut and the press release

Walter Haut was the Public Information Officer for the Roswell Base at the time in question. He was instructed by Colonel Blanchard to put out a press release at the time of the incident which read as follows:

Roswell Army Air Base, Roswell, N.M. 8 July 1947, a.m.

The many rumours regarding the flying disc became a reality yesterday when the intelligence office of the 509th Bomb Group of the Eighth Air Force, Roswell Army Air Field, was fortunate enough to gain possession of a disc through the co-operation of one of the local ranchers and the sheriff's office of Chaves Country.

The flying object landed on a ranch near Roswell some time last week. Not having phone facilities, the rancher stored the disc until such time as he was able to contact the sheriff's office, who in turn notified Major Jesse A. Marcel of the 509th Bomb Group Intelligence Office.

Action was immediately taken and the disc was picked up at the rancher's home. It was inspected at the Roswell Army Air Field and subsequently loaned by Major Marcel to higher headquarters.

This press release appeared across the US and in some publications abroad, until it was refuted by General Ramey of Fort Worth who said in a radio hook-up that no such thing as a flying disc was known to the army 'at least not at this level'. As we know, interest was not halted by this statement, and this marked the start of speculation and investigation that are still continuing over half a century later.

Haut, himself a practising Christian and stalwart of his local church, described security at the Roswell Base in 1947 as being very tight. It however was a priority with the military there to foster good relations with the local community, including the newspaper. Haut cannot

remember whether he wrote the press release himself or whether he was given the words by Colonel Blanchard, but he states that he did have the authorization of the colonel. However, he also believed that the real authority must have come from higher up, due to the sensitive and extreme import of the disclosure about a 'flying disc'. Haut feels the whole thing must have been orchestrated, so that the local base put out the controversial information only to have it quashed from higher up, saying the locals didn't know any better and that the thing was just a new type of weather balloon. Had they immediately called it a weather balloon it would have been much harder to convince people, because the material was not the same as the usual weather balloon construction. Having allowed the press release about the flying disc to go out, it was somehow easier then to write the wreckage off as a new type of balloon.

If Haut's opinion is correct, this would make the Roswell incident the subject of the first disinformation on UFOs. It does indeed seem strange in the first place that the military would issue so definitive a press release about a flying disc being captured, without thoroughly checking the material, and it is one of the many details of the Roswell incident that does not add up.

Project Mogul

The latest official explanation for the Roswell incident (and one that has convinced many people) concerns another type of balloon, engaged in 'Project Mogul'. This was a top-secret project designed to measure signs in the atmosphere of Soviet nuclear tests, and was accomplished by long-range low-frequency acoustic devices, borne by balloons. It was a highly classified matter at the time, as the Cold War was beginning to take hold and those involved in the project did not, as a rule, know about the whole matter, but just the portion for which they had responsibility. Various types of balloon were experimented with. Many flights were launched, using a variety of equipment. Radar targets were used for tracking balloons because they did not at first have all the necessary equipment for what was then an advanced endeavour. Some of the radar targets were made

by a toy company, using aluminium foil, balsa wood coated with special glue to make it durable, braided nylon twine, brass eyelets and swivels to make a reflector; something like a box kite. A pink tape with symbols on it was also used on occasion.

Flights of balloons were made from 20 November 1946 to 2 July 1947 by neoprene meteorological balloons, in contrast to later flights which were with polyethylene balloons. Professor Moore of Project Mogul stated that these neoprene balloons degraded in the sunlight, turning from white to brown, so they would look like ashes strewn in the desert, while the chemicals in the neoprene would emit an acrid smell – both elements correspond to descriptions of material found at the Roswell crash site. Moore believes that the balloon that crashed was probably Service Flight 4, launched on 4 June 1947, and not recovered by members of the project. This opinion is endorsed by Colonel Cavitt, the only living witness to the crashed material, who was with Major Marcel at the time of the recovery. Cavitt, who is regarded by many UFO researchers as being closed-mouthed and somewhat mysterious, feels that he has often been misrepresented. He claims that he has never been sworn to secrecy, and that he always felt the debris was that of a crashed balloon. In fact, he claims not to have known that anything noteworthy happened in the summer of 1947 at Roswell, until interviewed in the early 1980s by researchers.

So that, presumably, is that. The great saucer incident deflated and was explained as being just a crashed balloon from Project Mogul. On the face of it, this would seem to be the end of the story, and for many researchers, sceptics and the American Air Force, it is. However, there are still some factors that do not add up. If Colonel Cavitt was with Jesse Marcel when they found the wreckage, why was there no discussion, no argument about the nature of the find? With Marcel so intent on an extra-terrestrial explanation, surely his colleague would have demurred. Surely there would be an official record of disagreement on an important matter such as this, and a delay in the press release while Colonel Blanchard considered the facts? Another point to consider is that while the purposes of Project Mogul were very special, the balloons used were not particularly esoteric or advanced.

Don Montoya, Public Information Officer for White Sands (one of the controversial and secret test sites, where German technology was developed after World War II) has searched the available records for evidence that a rocket or balloon from the White Sands Base was launched at a time when it could have been involved in the Roswell incident. No balloons were launched during the month in question and all the rockets were accounted for – in any case, no contemporary rocket could have reached that far. Despite repeated searches of the records for that time, no further information has come to light. Tim Shawcross describes Montoya as also unconvinced by the Project Mogul explanation. He quotes him (see Further reading) as saying:

> *"There had been some balloon tests that did come out of Alamogordo but once again we did have the records for 1947 and they showed no incidents of any kind of balloons straying off towards that area. As far as White Sands is concerned, we're pretty clean on this incident."*

The descriptions of the neoprene balloons and their radar targets do indeed tally with some of the data given by people who saw the Roswell debris, and yet a 'clean case' can still not be said to have been arrived at. A more far-fetched, but ultimately possible, scenario is that an alien craft somehow got tangled with a balloon and they came down together. Some writers have asserted that a craft of presumably advanced technology could surely avoid mishaps and crashes. However, unless we presume the pilots to be infallible, it must be possible even for them to have accidents. We do not know what their propulsion methods might be. If they use the forces of anti-gravity, magnetism, electricity and such, (and if, indeed, these craft exist at all) it may indeed be possible, under freak conditions, for them to come down, all controls disrupted by electromagnetic disturbance. In the early years of the Cold War, in the feverish, paranoid atmosphere, many tests were being undertaken in secret, and Nazi war criminals escaped detention because they were prepared to help in scientific tests for the Americans (and presumably for other countries, too). At bases such as Alamogordo, Roswell and others, there were many sightings of unidentified craft by trained military personnel any by eminent scientists. Does this not make sense? If 'they' were concerned for us, for whatever

reason, would 'they' not have been especially observant at those very places where experimentation into globally threatening and very novel means of destruction were being researched? I think so. I also think it is possible that those involved in any way with these alarming new methods, would have felt very uneasy, at some level, about what they were doing. In an age when God is no longer taken seriously by most people, what better agency on which to project fear of retribution than the 'flying saucers'?

The alien autopsy

No discussion of Roswell would be complete without an examination of the supposed 'alien autopsy' film. While this film is considered to be almost definitely a hoax, there is still the 'almost'. No definite proof that this film has been faked has yet come to light, and it adds further to the mystery of the entire event.

This film was unleashed upon the world in 1994, by small-business man Ray Santilli, owner of a video distribution company. It is a black and white film showing an autopsy performed on alien creatures, recovered from a spaceship that crashed in New Mexico in 1947. It is about 15 minutes in length and shows two people covered from head to toe in one-piece white garments, complete with hoods and visors. Such suits are standard apparel for those who have to deal with nuclear or chemical contaminants. The two approach a corpse, lying prone on a wheeled hospital bed, take scalpels and other instruments from a tray, and carry out a dissection on the body. The photography is very unclear, showing the internal organs as amorphous blobs although the creature itself is of humanoid appearance and thus might have been expected to have insides at least a little like our own. The entire film is the work of one cameraman, and so the shots all come from a similar angle, and are indistinct. The creature being dissected is similar to the many descriptions of aliens. It is small, has a large hairless head and almond-shaped eyes. Its arms are long, and it has six fingers and six toes. A Y-shaped cut is made at the start of the autopsy, around the neck and shoulder-blades. The 'organs' extracted are

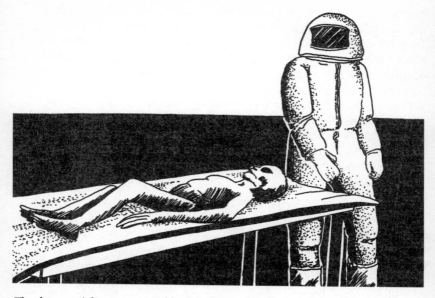

The famous 'alien autopsy' film has been a source of controversy, with ufologists unable to authenticate it or to dismiss it completely.

placed on a steel hospital tray and taken to one side. Forensic pathologist Dr West of Scotland Yard could not fault the medical technique used, and while he professed that he was almost certain he was looking at some sort of hoax, he also admitted that it could be real. Other people have been very critical of the techniques displayed in the film.

Special effects experts have pronounced the film a fake, but as almost anything can indeed be faked on film, it is hard to see on what they might base this judgment, other than the general improbability of the subject. Such a film would have been difficult to make, and very costly, requiring a team effort with everyone sworn to secrecy, which is possible, of course. Not surprisingly, Santilli insists that the film is genuine and that he came by it while searching for footage of Elvis in concert, at a convention in the USA. The autopsy film was offered to him by someone who stated that he

had been an official military cameraman in 1947, in Washington DC, and that he had been flown to New Mexico in 1947 to film a crashed spaceship, on a top-secret mission. He had kept some pieces of the film separate, because they needed special attention in developing, due to the lighting, and these had never been collected from him. This was possibly because at the time in question the army and the air force were in the process of separating into two distinct forces. Certainly, and interestingly, it is true that the relevant records, at the time of the Roswell incident, have indeed 'gone missing'. The cameraman has rigorously protected his identity, because he is supposedly afraid of reprisal, and Santilli has been sworn to secrecy. Some might say this is convenient.

In the summer of 1947 the cameraman was flown to Roswell and then driven to the 'site', where he says a large disc had crashed, and heat was still radiating from it. Several creatures were lying near the craft, each holding a box close to its chest, and screaming. Someone managed to take one of the boxes away by hitting the creature with a rifle-butt (a great start to interplanetary relations!). The cameraman was filming the site as all that happened. At length the creatures and the debris were taken away. Most of the debris seemed to have come from exterior parts, supporting a smaller disc on the underside of the craft. Three days later the decision was taken to remove the entire craft, and so it was taken back to Wright Paterson. Inside the craft the atmosphere was very heavy and sickening. The cameraman went to Wright Paterson along with the recovered saucer and the three weeks later he filmed the 'autopsy'. However, due to the risk of contamination, he had to wear protective clothing while filming, hence the poor quality of the footage. Amazingly, despite being told that some of the film was held back by the cameraman for special processing, no-one ever collected it.

Santilli's story contains inconsistencies, which he has plausibly explained away, sometimes on the grounds of protecting confidentiality. Despite promises, no sample of the original 16mm film has been produced to be tested for age and other telling characteristics. No human on the film is identifiable, because the faces are never visible. Consultation with known and identified military cameramen at the time of the Roswell incident indicates

that the procedures surrounding the 'film' were most irregular. For instance, skilled cameramen with the necessary clearance were available much closer to the 'site' and so it is unlikely that a 12-hour delay, to fly someone in from Washington would have been countenanced. Furthermore, all such filming was subject to the very strict regulations and the cameraman never developed his own film. In addition, all the film had to be carefully accounted for – the idea of bits just not being collected is ludicrous. Furthermore, autopsies were filmed in colour, not black and white, as the 'alien autopsy' film appears, and they were filmed by two cameras, one of which would be placed at ceiling height to obtain overhead shots. Only one camera is used for the film in question, and there is no 'stills' cameraman visible in the footage. This also would have been most irregular, as still shots were always taken and the photographer would obviously feature in the motion picture, In addition, autopsy filming was always of the highest quality and clarity, because of its importance. This does not match up with the atrocious quality of the alien autopsy footage, where the camera work is exceptionally poor. Experts are of the opinion that under the circumstances, the clarity should have been exceptionally good, and that the film has, in fact, been made purposely obscure. Finally, the identity of the cameraman was kept secret in order to protect him. Surely it would hardly matter whether anyone knew his name or not, because if he really were engaged in something so secret, those who had employed him would know the identity of the informant in an instant.

It does seem very doubtful that the alien autopsy film is genuine, yet as far as I am aware it has not definitely been proved to be a fraud, and while the experts involved in assessing it are not impressed, it has not been unequivocally and universally denounced. Several possibilities exist, in addition to the likelihood of a hoax. One is the very nasty idea that the US government was engaged in some experimentation on humans, and while this is hardly to be contemplated, they have nevertheless been implicated in unauthorized experiments on humans with radiation and drugs. This might explain all the rumours of 'alien' corpses. However, it still does not really explain the controversial film.

Another, more viable, possibility is that some maverick or highly-secret department carried out the autopsies and filmed them without the knowledge of the rest of the armed forces or government. Here we confront that old conspiracy theory again. In support of this an FBI memo exists, dated 19 August 1947, dealing with the subject of flying discs. This document reveals that a special agent, in discussion with a lieutenant colonel, (the names are blacked out on the document) was told that it was possible that the flying discs were part of a highly classified experiment on the part of the army or the navy, that the colonel's personal opinion was that this was the case, and that this was supported by the views of an eminent scientist (whose name, is, of course, blacked out). The colonel made the point that while much interest was shown in flying objects spotted over Sweden by the War Department, similar sightings over home territory had been shrugged off, although many sightings were reported by trained observers who were highly credible witnesses. If these phenomena really are familiar to the government, any FBI investigation could be very embarrassing indeed. The memo names two generals who had given assurance that the army was not involved and a resolution is arrived at, to ask for a memo from the Research and Development Corps in the air force to specify whether any experiments were being carried out that would coincide with the observed phenomena. It is not clear whether this memo ever arrived.

While it passes belief that the 'alien autopsy' footage could be an example of 'ordinary' top-secret filming, it is surely not impossible that this is indeed a record of something more secret than secret, on the part of a person or persons unknown, in the military or government. Or is that too paranoid a fantasy?

The elusive truth

Despite all the evidence, discussion, speculation, claims and counter-claims, it seems we still have little idea what happened at Roswell in the early days of July 1947. All we know is that some debris was recovered and that we are not being, and have not been, told the truth, the whole truth and nothing but the truth.

An FBI document, now available under the Freedom of Information Act, is dated the same day as the Roswell Press Release. It is a teletype from FBI Dallas to Cincinnati, and concerns the recovery of a purported 'flying disc' near Roswell. The 'disc' was apparently hexagonal in shape and suspended from a balloon 20ft (6m) in diameter. While this resembled a weather balloon, communication with Wright Field (earlier known as Wright Paterson) had not borne this out, and the object was being transported by special plane to Wright Field for examination. Wright Field were to be requested to advise Cincinnati of the results of the investigation, and no further investigation was to be conducted.

As we are all too well aware, this was just the start of the matter, as far as many UFO researchers were concerned. For my own part, I have to say that for many years I have been inclined to believe the UFO 'myth', that an alien craft really did crash near Roswell, New Mexico, in 1947, and the details of this were concealed by the authorities, for whatever nefarious reasons. Now, having looked into the matter more closely, I am not so sure. Everything is too vague and questionable, and for me what especially raises doubt is the matter of the pink tape mentioned earlier in this chapter, with markings on it, which turns out to very similar to materials used in Project Mogul (and doesn't sound very extra-terrestrial).

Perhaps one day evidence will come to light that gives a final explanation for the Roswell incident. Until that time, each one of us must make up our own minds, or preferably decide to keep them open.

3

the philadelphia experiment

'Curiouser and curiouser' cried Alice.

Alice's Adventures in Wonderland, Lewis Caroll (1832–1898)

The 'Philadelphia Experiment' is the name given to an experiment believed to have been carried out by the US Navy, in 1943, where a destroyer, the USS Eldridge, disappeared from its berth in Philadelphia, to reappear at almost the same time in Norfolk, Virginia. Soon after this the ship rematerialized in its original place, with disastrous consequences for the crew. At the time the US and Europe were at war with Nazi Germany, and it is certain that experiments on the fringes of science were indeed being carried out in order to develop a weapon that would decisively win the war for the Allies. The outcome, as we well know, was the making of the atom bomb. The rest, as they say, is history.

However, the Philadelphia Experiment is not accepted history, but rests on hearsay. No official records have been found of this matter, and its name was given by researchers into the mystery, not by officials. Nevertheless, the rumours have not died, and it would appear that something needs to be explained. There is something about the whole affair that has obsessed several investigators, and even destroyed lives. While many of the descriptions are fantastical, not to mention highly alarming, speculation is based on several facts. Firstly, reports exist concerning the incident, although some are somewhat dubious. Secondly, at the time, in the mid-twentieth century, the power of science was making itself felt, and there is no doubt that attempts were being made to create a 'super-weapon', in

The compelling case of the post-war Philadelphia Experiment continues to baffle and enthral researchers to this day.

all probability connected with the new view of energy and matter revealed by Einstein's Theory of Relativity. This theory did, in fact, lead to the creation of the atom bomb. Thirdly, Einstein's unproved Unified Field Theory would seem to support the possibility of the kind of phenomena observed in the ill-fated Philadelphia Experiment.

All of this is relevant to the study of UFOs because the elements of the 'experiment' – invisibility, anti-gravity, alternative dimensions – are connected to the apparent abilities and behaviour patterns of UFOs. In addition, UFOs were reported to have been spotted in the vicinity at the time of the alleged experiment. Those involved in it were reported to have seen aliens and UFOs. Reports and speculation on the matter go far beyond this, with theories being put forward suggesting the use of alien technology, co-operation with aliens and continuing forays in space/time. Let us begin at the beginning.

Dr Jessup

Morris Ketchum Jessup was born in Indiana on 20 March 1900. His adolescence coincided with World War I, and on his graduation he enlisted in the US Armed Forces. After the war, he set about acquiring an extensive education in several sciences, namely astrophysics, astronomy and mathematics, which enabled him to lecture at several US universities. In the late 1920s, while studying for his doctorate, he had the opportunity to travel to South America to work with the largest contemporary refracting telescope, in Bloemfontein, Orange Free State. His work here resulted in the cataloguing of a number of double stars. Later this work was used for his doctoral dissertation, and while it is not clear that he was ever formally awarded this title, those who knew him referred to him as Dr Jessup. There is no doubt that he was a scientist and academic of sound reputation and ability.

During the 1930s, when money and scientific posts were in short supply, Jessup was involved in expeditions to the jungles of South America. Here he seems to have had new and original thoughts, inspired by the Inca ruins, and the cyclopean stones that formed

them. He came to the conclusion that these structures had been created in remote times by an advanced, antediluvian civilization, possessing some sort of anti-gravity device that was operated from sky-born vessels. Jessup had now entered the academic and scientific hinterland and his career was imperiled. Continuing his investigations under his own steam, Jessup was drawn to examine certain craters in Mexico, which seemed to bear a remarkable resemblance to similar craters on the surface of the moon. These, he came to suggest, had been made by craft from space, and he revealed at a later date that the US Air Force possessed aerial photographs of the area in question and that the matter was classified. By now it was the early 1950s and funds were depleted, so Dr Jessup went home to try to raise money for more exploration. The age of the 'flying saucer' had dawned, and Jessup speculated that this phenomenon was linked to the ancient relics and strange craters, so making him one of the first proponents of the Ancient Astronaut Theory. He felt some principle of anti-gravity was in operation, and he began work on a book, entitled *The Case for the UFO* (Citadel Press, 1955).

Jessup's motivation for this work had been, to some extent, to raise funds for his explorations. However, the publication of his book was to set more strange events in motion. In *The Case for the UFO* he appealed for more research to be undertaken into anti-gravity, pointing out that while humans were reliant on primitive rocket power, they were effectively earth-bound. Jessup's book enjoyed some success, provoking correspondence from a certain Señor Carlos Allende, and it is on this mysterious and ambiguous correspondence that the principle evidence for the Philadelphia Experiment rests. (This is explored further in the following section.) The letters were remarkable – mis-spelled, with capital letters and underlining all over the place, and using several different colours of ink. Despite this, the first letter interested Jessup to the point where he wondered whether the writer knew something specific about anti-gravity and its use by the ancients, and he replied to it. Meanwhile his second book *UFO and the Bible* was in preparation. He was lecturing widely, stressing to his audiences the necessity for funds to be channelled into research on anti-gravity on the basis of the

Unified Field Theory, in order to make space travel possible, and economical. It was some while before another letter from the same correspondent arrived through his door, and when it did it seemed apparent that Allende had been present at one lecture, at least.

The second letter outlined the horrendous details of an experiment that had been carried out by the navy, which had resulted in a ship 'disappearing' and the sailors on board becoming partially or totally invisible. The writer was even abusive to Jessup for encouraging research in what he considered a very dangerous area. Nonetheless, further letters arrived, offering more details and help, even suggesting that Allende submit to hypnosis in order to recover forgotten data about the incident. At first Jessup was naturally sceptical, but gradually he came to wonder whether there might be a germ of truth here, for he knew there had been many classified experiments carried out by the military at the time in question. However, Jessup was hoping for funding for another expedition to Mexico, and it is probable that he would have written the whole thing off as fantastical when events took a further turn. A copy of Jessup's first book, *The Case for the UFO* was sent to Major Ritter, Aeronautical Project Officer at the Office of Naval Research. There was no accompanying letter, but the work itself was covered in scrawl about UFOs and their propulsion systems, etc. The notes gave explanations for the disappearances in the Bermuda Triangle and elsewhere, and for other phenomena such as strange objects falling from the sky, undersea civilizations, force fields, telepathy and many other subjects. Clearly the writer knew, or thought he knew a great deal about the UFO phenomenon. It is unclear why Major Ritter preserved the book. However, it was later passed on to two other officers at the Office of Naval Research who were currently involved in a secret project to launch the first satellite, and who were also interested in anti-gravity. These men contacted Jessup and showed him the annotated copy of his book.

Jessup was disquieted both by the extensive knowledge displayed by the annotator and by the navy's interest. He soon realized that the notes in the book and the peculiar letters he had received originated from the same person, Carlos Allende. Jessup passed the letters on to Commander Hoover who arranged for Jessup's book to be

reprinted, with the inclusion of the notes and the Allende letters. Why this was done is not really clear, although the book was circulated in Washington military circles and the officers concerned, Commander Hoover and Captain Sherby, wrote in the introduction of the importance of discovering the nature of gravity. Quite what was going on in the mind of Jessup is hard to imagine, but he spent a lot of time going over the annotated copy of his book, making his own exhaustive notes. Meanwhile, the navy tried to track down Allende, without success. Why, if nothing was going on, were the navy going to all these lengths? This question must have been in Jessup's mind, along with the haunting descriptions of the 'experiment' itself given in the Allende letters. Jessup's private life was falling apart and he became very depressed.

With no money forthcoming for research, Jessup pursued his writing career and became interested in psychic phenomena. Towards the end of October 1958, Jessup was a guest at the home of his friend, the naturalist Ivan T. Sanderson. He gave the original re-annotated copy of his book to one of the company to be kept safe, in case anything should happen to him. His friends, some of whom were psychics, felt very disturbed about what was happening, for the matter had an unpleasant 'feel'. Many inexplicable things, odd coincidences, were taking place in his life. His scientific interests had apparently drawn him into a tangled web of peculiar, inexplicable happenings. Jessup feared he would be regarded as insane, although he did not truly think he was, and he had the strong sensation that things couldn't go on much longer without something happening. Because of this, Jessup asked a friend to guard the book, in order that it could not be accidentally discovered by people who would say he had gone mad. Jessup did not want that stigma to alight on his children and grandchildren.

Subsequently, Jessup had a serious car accident, and is on record as having written very depressed notes to those who knew him. Jessup, in the spring of 1959, was 59, and at a very low ebb. He spent considerable time with another friend, Dr Valentine, who was a scientist, archaelogist and investigator of the Bermuda Triangle. Jessup confided to Valentine many of his thoughts and feelings about the Philadelphia Experiment. On 20 April 1959, the two friends

spoke and Valentine invited Jessup to dinner. He accepted, but never turned up. At 6.30 p.m. he was found, almost dead, from self-inflicted carbon-monoxide poisoning, slumped over the wheel of his car, not far from his home, the exhaust pipe connected to a hose which had been inserted through the passenger window. Very shortly after, he died. Because Jessup had bequeathed his body for scientific research no autopsy was ever performed. Valentine revealed that Jessup had been approached by the navy to continue working on anti-gravity, but he was too worried by the implications and so he declined. He had been depressed, it is true, but Valentine suggested that perhaps he had, in fact been allowed to die. Later, it came to light from the medical examiner's files, that Jessup's blood, at the time of death, contained a lethal concentration of alcohol, to the extent that it would have been quite impossible for him even to get into a car, let alone drive it several miles, write a suicide note and connect up the hose to the exhaust.

Valentine believed that Jessup knew a great deal about the true facts of the Philadelphia Experiment, being a distinguished and respected scientist. The 'experiment' was an actuality, and was accomplished by using magnetic generators pulsed at frequencies calculated to create a strong magnetic field around a ship. This magnetic resonance caused the ship to slip out of the present dimension, in effect becoming transferred to another level of reality. More specifically, two magnetic fields at right angles to each other are created by a coil, thus representing two dimensions of space. However, because there are three dimensions, a third field is needed, possibly a gravitational one. This might be created through resonance, by means of magnetic generators emitting a magnetic pulse. On the basis of information received from Jessup, Valentine recounted how at the commencement of the experiment the vessel was surrounded by a green misty glow until it permeated the ship and the crew began to disappear. Eventually, all that was left was the impression of the ship's hull in the water. Jessup told Valentine that he believed the navy had stumbled on this. A notable point about the entire operation was how badly it had affected the human beings caught in the generated field.

Señor Carlos Allende

The most graphic accounts of the 'experiment' originate with Carlos Allende, or Carl Allen, a merchant seaman, whose origins may have been Irish or Spanish. Because Allende appears to have been eccentric, and with a dubious past, one could dismiss his letters as the ravings of a lunatic, were it not for additional information that has come to light.

Allende asserted that Einstein's Unified Field Theory was not 'incomplete' but totally workable, but that the navy was afraid of it, for good reason, because they had already used magnetic fields with terrible results. The 'field' had been experimented with, in the shape of an oblate spheroid, upon a ship at sea. According to Allende, all people on board the ship became vague in form and many of the crew suffered distressing after-effects. His descriptions are confusing, and it sounds as if he is talking about several experiments or extensive experiments repeated over a period of time. He claimed to have witnessed at least some of the experiments while at sea on board the SS Andrew Feruseth, along with certain comrades. He also claimed to know that the 'navy boss' was very enthusiastic about the experiments. Allende supplied his merchant navy number to Jessup in his correspondence.

The Unified Field Theory

Despite the discoveries of Einstein, we still live, conceptually, in a Newtonian universe, where everything moves like clockwork. We have not fully embraced the idea of relativity, or that matter and energy are, essentially, the same thing. The basic idea behind this is perhaps more generally accepted in New Age thought, often expressed in what could be called a woolly fashion, in terms of 'vibes' and 'energies'. Science generally, however, seems to maintain a strictly conventional and solid approach. Sadly, the circumstance most galvanizing to the imagination is often war, and at the time of World War II, Einstein had gravitated to America, horrified at the excesses of the Nazis. He brought with him his Unified Field Theory.

The Unified Field Theory argues that gravity, electricity and magnetism are inextricably linked. When fields are 'unified' it means that if you alter one, you alter the other. Because of this it could, theoretically, be possible to control and manipulate the force of gravity. However, the effects of this may go much further. If these three forces are the strands that 'glue' our reality in place, start fiddling with them and more may happen than was bargained for. Light, space and possibly time itself may be altered. Space could be 'folded', enabling light years to be travelled in an instant. Scientists have proved that gravity bends light because of the effects of the sun on the light from the stars behind it – even though these stars are known to be 'behind' the sun at a given point in the year, they can still be seen. Theoretically, it could be possible to 'wrap' an object in bent light, so that it became invisible.

While the Philadelphia Experiment is on the fringes of science, it is not outside the realms of current scientific theory. To dismiss anti-gravity, invisibility and even interdimensional travel as 'impossible' is merely to take up the 'ostrich position' – heads in the sand. In Philadelphia in 1943, a ship and its crew could indeed have been made invisible, with dramatic and disastrous ramifications.

An incomplete version of the Unified Field Theory was published in Prussian scientific journals in the 1920s. It was withdrawn, rather strangely, by the pacifist Einstein and made no reappearance until close to the time of the alleged 'experiment' in Philadelphia. Bertrand Russell, also a pacifist, was a close friend of Einstein's and is reported by one of his biographers to have seen information on new weapons technology, classified as top secret by British Intelligence, just after World War II. This is said to have shocked him so deeply that he pressed for a world peace manifesto, which was signed by Einstein.

Einstein is believed to have burned some of his papers before his death. At the time of the Philadelphia Experiment, Einstein was a scientific consultant to the US Navy, and his activities were somewhat secret. Less than two years before his death, Einstein told of convincing results in his attempts to find mathematical proof connecting electromagnetism and gravity. If this has been taken further, the results have not been made public.

further corroboration

Allende asserts that a ship called the USS Eldridge was involved in the experiment, in Philadelphia, in October 1943. If this is the case, one might expect the ship's records to confirm at least the position of the ship at the time in question. Interestingly, these records have been 'lost'. Records do prove that one Carl Allen was indeed aboard the Fusureth in October 1943. In fact the war-time 'action records' show that the Fusureth and the Eldridge were in the same convoy in November 1943, off North Africa. Existing records are a garbled mishmash, suggesting that something may indeed have been covered up, however, this does not prove exactly what it could have been.

In the Allende letters a certain Dr Franklin Reno is mentioned as being in charge of a recheck of the Unified Field Theory. Researchers failed, for many years, to track down this possibly fictional figure, because his name was an alias, assumed for protection. However, the researcher William Moore, co-author of *The Philadelphia Experiment: Project Invisibility* (see Further reading) reports locating the man in question, who is still protected by an alias. This pivotal figure, let us call him Dr R, did indeed describe war-time conferences on the Unified Field Theory and its uses. These included Einstein and a Professor Ladenburg from Switzerland, who had been working on fission experiments. Ladenburg and Einstein had consulted together regarding the use of electromagnetic fields to counter mines and torpedoes. This extended to a project to induce optical invisibility, as a defensive measure. Dr R, Because of his speed in computation, was asked to work on some last-minute calculations, regarding bending light around a ship. A high-level and speedy project was in place within the Naval Defence Research Committee, concerning force-fields, and no copies were permitted of the relevant material. Dr R's memory is hazy about the code-name of the project, believing it may have been 'Rainbow' or 'Mirage'. Dr R specifically mentions Admiral Land as being approached for a ship for the experiment, possibly with hand-picked and experienced sailors. So the testimony of Dr R would seem, quite unambiguously, to support the basic supposed facts of the Philadelphia Experiment.

One might legitimately ask how it could be that no-one has invented an anti-gravity machine, if the supporting scientific theories are already in place. The answer is that they have. In the early part of the twentieth century Townsend Brown was working on X-rays. He felt that, because of the thrust they induced in a tube when switched on, they might hold the secret of space travel. Later he discovered that the power came from the high-voltage electricity used to generate the rays. On the basis of this he built a 'gravitor', a small plastic box containing a high-voltage tube. When he switched it on it lost about one per cent of its weight, thus obliterating some of the force of gravity, albeit a small part. When Brown first discovered this he was only a schoolboy, and no-one took him seriously. However, Brown, though a quiet person, was as tenacious as he was gifted.

In 1930 Brown joined the Naval Research Laboratory in Washington DC and by 1939 he was a lieutenant in the Navy Reserve. Dr R stated that he became involved with the 'experiment' when he was brought into the Bureau of Ships in charge of acoustic and magnetic minesweeping. Brown is also believed to have put forward suggestions for partial radar invisibility, achievable through the use of electromagnetic fields. Brown was a hard worker, but personal disappointments and the failure to gain recognition for his projects brought him low, and in the winter of 1943 he suffered a breakdown and was sent home to rest. This is a telling date, but there is no proof of Brown's direct involvement in the Philadelphia Experiment, if such an experiment did take place.

After the war, Brown became very interested in UFOs and he thought that scientists should look into how they might be powered. He tried to obtain government funding for his gravitor. Despite its demonstrable success, no support was forthcoming. Brown believed in an identifiable and observable coupling effect between electricity and gravity, in keeping with the Unified Field Theory. He worked ceaselessly on his gravitor until it was impressive indeed. By 1952 it was powerful enough to lift more than its own weight. Then he went on to power disc-shaped models, flying around the circular course at 19kmph (12mph). Interestingly, these gave off a bluish glow and a low humming noise, just like the reports of 'flying saucers'. These results were immediately classified – but not developed by the

government. Some sources assert that this is because the government already had these capabilities, passed on to them by aliens with whom they were already in contact.

Brown went to Europe to try to sell his ideas, but the company who decided to buy his research were taken over by another company who, for some unknown reason, refused to proceed with the experiments. Back in the USA a rich business man offered to back Brown and his gravitor, but the business man died in a plane crash, in circumstances which appeared suspicious. Subsequently, Brown created his own company, called Rand International, but despite numerous successful demonstrations and the granting of patents, all support simply dissolved around Brown and his invention.

We can only wonder, did someone not want us to have the benefits of anti-gravity? And could that be because they knew that the 'benefits' are not worth the risks? Or is there some even more bizarre explanation involving collaboration with aliens? The career of Townsend Brown does seem to have been dogged by more than ill luck.

More anecdotes

A report exists originating with an erstwhile security guard who was watching over classified, audiovisual material, in 1945. At this time, while on duty in Washington, he was able to watch a film, along with many high-ranking officials from the navy. Although he did not see the whole film, he saw snatches of it. It showed three ships, two of which appeared to be beaming energy, possibly sound waves, at the third ship. After a while the ship concerned disappeared into a kind of fog, leaving only the impression of the shape of its hull in the waves. When the generators were switched off the ship came back into view. Some of the watching naval officers were heard to remark that perhaps the power had been left on for too long, and that affected the crew. One of them stated that certain sailors had been seen to disappear while having a drink in a bar, some were not in their right minds and would never recover and others had disappeared without trace. This account has some notable

similarities with the Allende accounts, although the security guard had no knowledge of him. However, this account is unverifiable, the name of the security guard being given only as 'Jim'.

Another rather disturbing fact is that the people involved with investigation into the Philadelphia Experiment seem to have died in rather dubious circumstances, or to have gone missing. One woman who allegedly had an affair with a crew member from the Eldridge said how he suffered strange symptoms and was rushed to hospital by the Navy. The woman herself became very depressed and died in an 'accident'. James Wolfe, a former navy man and freelance writer also went missing while writing a book on the subject. And of course, we now know the circumstances surrounding the death of Dr Jessup. Because of this it is hardly surprising that people who supply information decline to be named. Sadly, this does not help to establish the authenticity of the entire affair, but it is understandable. In *The Philadelphia Experiment* (see Further reading) one of Charles Berlitz's informants 'who emphatically declined to be named, confided … that he had seen highly classified documents in the Navy files in Washington DC, which indicated that at least some phases of the experiments are STILL in progress'.

In 1970, two airmen called Allen Huse and James Davis were out walking in the War Memorial Park in Colorado Springs when they were approached by a somewhat abstracted character. This man struck up a friendly conversation, and revealed that he had been in the navy but that he had been pensioned off due to mental instability because they had done 'things' to him. He said he had been involved in an invisibility experiment, which had done bad things to the crew of the ship on which the experiment was carried out. The man spoke of having had the choice as to whether he joined a top-secret experiment in Philadelphia, and said that he wished, with hindsight, that he had not volunteered. He said that some sort of energy fields had been used, and that the crew had been affected in different ways; some saw double; some laughed and staggered; some said they had passed into another world and had talked with alien beings. In some cases effects persisted after the experiment. Some apparently died later, others were pensioned off as disabled, after being put away for a few months to 'rest' while attempts were made to persuade them it never happened

and to swear them to secrecy. Again, this is an account that cannot be substantiated, because the name of the ex-seaman was never given. Perhaps he was a tortured individual who needed to unburden himself to fellow servicemen, understandably protecting his identity. Or perhaps he had lost his mind.

This story, if true, might indicate that contact was made with another world during the Philadelphia Experiment, and if this is the case, possibly the reason for the 'cover-up' is that the contact is still in progress. This may sound far-fetched, but certain official reactions to a UFO incident lend credence to the view. On 7 October 1975, in Bracebridge, Ontario, Robert Suffren went to investigate a strange glow in a barn, near his sister's house. Finding nothing remarkable in the barn, Suffern proceeded to his sister's only to find a saucer-shaped object, about 14ft (4¼m) in diameter, on the road ahead. Before he could stop, the object went straight upwards and out of sight. He turned for home and saw a humanoid creature in a silver suit and helmet. It jumped over a fence at the side of the road as if it was weightless. Suffern was very shaken by the incident, and when he got home he looked out of his window only to see the saucer-like object flying just over the road. Again, it zoomed upwards and disappeared. Suffern and his family were besieged by reporters, but it was nine months later when he and his wife, almost reluctantly revealed some interesting facts. It transpired that, after the initial furore of the UFO incident had subsided, certain high-ranking officials from the Canadian Forces and the Pentagon arrived at the Suffern's home. These men confirmed that the US and Canadian governments had known about the UFOs since 1943 (that telling year!) and had been co-operating with the extra-terrestrials since then! The officials apologized for the alarm caused by the 'mistake' on 7 October, which was due to a malfunction in the craft. The visitors knew details of the incident not formerly revealed to the media or to anyone else, and insisted that a UFO was involved, not a military, top-secret craft. Subsequent revelations described how contact was first made in 1943, after an accident involving a radar invisibility experiment, which made the forces aware of alien movements on earth.

Because of the Secrets Act, Suffern refused to disclose the names of the officers involved, giving loyalty as his reason for silence. It is interesting that an officer from the Office of Naval Intelligence was involved, bearing in mind this was a UFO case. The Sufferns were medically and psychologically checked before the alleged visit by the authorities concerned.

It is very hard to make anything coherent of this matter. Of course, it could be a fabrication on the part of the Sufferns. It could also be part of a process of 'testing' by the powers-that-be, of the effects of such disclosures on the public. Maybe this was part of a scheme to drip-feed information hitherto concealed about aliens, anti-gravity, invisibility, etc. to the public. And maybe it is simply true.

Anti-gravity and the bending of light are fact. Einstein's Unified Field Theory and his concern for the implications of the application of his discoveries are fact. War-time experiments in exotic weaponry are fact. The falsification of the records of the USS Eldridge is fact. The effects of electromagnetic fields on humans are known fact. An invisibility experiment can hardly be out of the question. Indeed, bearing in mind its implications for defence and the available scientific theory, it would almost have been surprising if it had not been entertained at some point.

ALIEN ACTIVITY

The only thing we have to fear is fear itself.

Franklin D. Roosevelt, Inaugural Address, 1933

The prospect of meeting up with beings from another world is perhaps the most exciting event that we can imagine for humanity, and one of the most frightening. We cannot know what attitude alien life forms may have towards us, and as it is likely that they will be technologically far in advance of us, their goodwill is necessary for our well-being and, possibly survival. It may be knowledge of our vulnerability that has given rise to unpleasant stories about alien activities or it could be morbid imagination at work. On the other hand, some of the stories might be true.

ABDUCTIONS

Abduction accounts are, for the most part, the most unacceptable side of the UFO phenomenon, but they are legion. A Roper Poll conducted in the US in the early 1990s indicated that possibly 3.7 million adult Americans may have had abduction experience. It would seem that belief in the extra-terrestrial hypothesis and in literal contact and abduction events is more popular in America, whereas the 'new ufology' of social and psychological explanations is favoured in more sceptical Europe, to the point where a type of 'UFO war' rages between proponents of the contending theories. Fundamentalism finds its way even into ufology!

PLEASANT ENCOUNTERS

There are those who report dealing with extremely seductive extra-terrestrials, and while such stories are the most incredible of all, they do at least endow the alien with a pleasant face – and body! Howard Menger, a sign-painter from New Jersey, had his close encounter in 1932, when he came across a landed saucer in a woodland. This alien was a gorgeous blonde, wearing a translucent suit that left little to the imagination. Menger had other contacts in Mexico, who informed him that the Mexicans were a favoured race and had been contacted before the arrival of the Spanish conquerors. More beautiful female aliens honoured Menger with a visit, and he was asked to provide them with a variety of earth-made objects, including a collection of brassieres for a saucer-load of beauties, who scornfully threw them back at him saying they didn't wear things like that where they came from! (So why ask for them?) This, and other events are detailed in Menger's book *From Outer Space To You* (Saucerian Books, 1959).

Perhaps the best known of the earlier contactees was George Adamski, who wrote *Flying Saucers Have Landed* (Neville Spearman, 1953) with Desmond Leslie, followed by *Inside the Spaceships* (Neville Spearman, 1955). Adamski's aliens were also stunningly attractive, hailing from Jupiter, Saturn, Venus and other planets, and he was fortunate enough to have discourse with a wise alien called 'The Master'. Adamski supported his stories with photographs (generally considered fakes) and he enjoyed popular acclaim on the talk-show circuit. Adamski's aliens were concerned for the human race and full of warnings about nuclear weapons.

A more up-to-date account concerns a British businessman, Mr W of Berkshire, England. Having badly injured his back in the 1960s, conventional medicine seemed unable to provide much help. Mr W had long been conscious of alien 'voices' inside his head, and in his desperation he 'reached out' to them. There followed the strangest episode imaginable, as his room filled with light and aliens lifted him from his bed, taking him into a type of operating theatre. Here he became aware that aliens were working on his back, although he

felt numb. Then he found himself back in bed, sitting upright and sweating profusely. The next day he was able to go back to work. Back trouble recurred in 1985 and he was sent for an X-ray in Heatherwood Hospital in Berkshire, where a team of experts subsequently questioned him about the operation on his back quite beyond the capabilities of current technology. Mr W has spent much of his own money trying to find out what has happened to him. Sceptics who choose to make much of the fact that Mr W heard 'voices' are still confronted by the physical evidence. (A full account of this can be found in *Amateur Astronomy & Earth Sciences* April/May 1996, written by Dave Goode.)

Unpleasant encounters

Stories of forced abductions, experiments and sexual abuse by aliens are very common indeed, and have even been incorporated into soap opera plots. A classic work on abduction is *Communion* by Whitley Strieber (see Further reading). This is written as a true account, although Strieber was a fiction writer. The book was an instant best-seller as it seemed to strike a chord with so many people, who, on reading the book, either recovered their own memories of abduction or felt a feeling of familiarity with the material and considerable unease.

Strieber recounts how a period of intense depression culminated in his recovering a memory of an alien encounter. He had awoken one night, unable to move. Entities came into his room and took him away to be operated on by small, grey-skinned beings. A contraption was inserted into his rectum, a needle was put into his skull, a cut was made in his finger (where an infection persists). Subsequent hypnotherapy recovered memories of other abductions throughout his life and these were corroborated by his wife, when she was regressed. *Communion* was followed by *Transformation* (William Morrow, 1988) where Strieber apparently comes more to terms with his experiences with the aliens. Strieber has been criticized by many people, who regard his work as fiction passed off as fact. Strieber's angle is that he became a writer of horror stories in the first place as

The sinister face of the Grey alien is a recurring feature in reports of alien encounters.

a kind of psychological defence mechanism. In fact he was telling the story of his own life.

One of the most famous abduction cases occurred on 19 September 1961, at 10.30 p.m. as Betty and Barney Hill were driving along Route 3 in New Hampshire. A bright object appeared in the sky, and although Barney argued that it was a plane, it came to rest in front of them, about 100 feet (30 metres) over the road. Getting out to investigate, Barney saw a row of bright portholes with alien faces looking out. He leapt back into his car and sped off, but the couple became conscious of a beeping sound, and became drowsy. They awoke to find their watches had stopped and they were many miles from their last remembered location. In the following days Betty had terrible nightmares which she became convinced were, in fact, memories. The couple both had hypnotherapy, and each recovered memories of being taken into a ship and operated upon. Betty underwent a 'pregnancy test' which involved the insertion of a long needle into her abdomen. Interestingly, Pease Air Force Base radar reported tracking an inexplicable craft over New Hampshire on the night in question. However, sceptics have criticized the story as being most unlikely and containing discrepancies and inconsistencies.

Even more distressing tales involve women who have been made pregnant by aliens, only to have their foetuses take from them. Certain reports tell of subsequent meetings with hybrid offspring, while the aliens tried to understand the bonding process. The human misery and distress involved here is unthinkable, whatever attitude one takes to the stories. The experience of Kathie Davis of Indianapolis is a case in point. A test prior to her wedding in 1978 confirmed her pregnancy, but later her periods returned as normal and another test proved negative. Hypnosis uncovered memories of abduction and an operation aboard an alien spacecraft where her foetus was removed. The baby had been the result of an alien fertilization. Months later she was taken again, to hold her baby which the aliens were rearing, because the aliens wished to learn about the human element and the importance of touch. Other memories also came flooding back, concerning the whole family, who had been subject to much interference by aliens who had landed in their back garden. An inexplicable burn mark on the ground testified

The famous abduction case of Betty and Barney Hill intrigued researchers by the similar reports they gave in separate hypnosis sessions.

to this, and Kathie had strange scars on her body. This tale is recounted in *Intruders* (Ballantine Books, 1988) by Budd Hopkins. Kathie's story is echoed by a large number of women with a similar tale to tell. Debunkers assert that there is no solid medical evidence for any of their claims.

Animal Mutilations

Perhaps one of the best known and most upsetting mutilation cases concerned Lady, a horse belonging to the sister of rancher Harry King, who offered grazing to the healthy young mare on his ranch in southern Colorado. At evening Lady would come back for water, but one evening, early in September 1967, she failed to appear. The next evening her carcass was found in a shocking state. From her shoulders to the tip of her nose all her flesh was gone, leaving a skull and spine that were bleached white, while the rest of the body was in a perfect state. A peculiar smell, like chlorine, hung about the body. A piece of something that looked like gizzard, with mane hair was found and this burnt the hand of the owner when she touched it. Pacific Ocean seaweed was discovered nearby and bushes close to the corpse had higher than normal levels of radiation.

Since then many thousands of cases have been reported and there may be even more we don't know about. Mutilations have been found in many parts of the world, although the phenomenon is mostly North American. Incidents are fairly similar in nature and share unpleasant characteristics. For instance, blood and body fluids are drained, genitals, and often an ear or eye, are missing, the rectum of the animal is cored, the tongue removed and the jawbone cut out and bleached. Occasionally brains have been removed without any sign of the skull being cut into and organs have been taken out of the body with no incision. A rancher, Emilio Lobato, lost 49 heads from his cattle in this manner. The interesting, and very disquieting thing is the surgical precision with which these mutilations are carried out. There are none of the characteristic signs that would normally be left by predators, such as teeth-marks, blood and remnants. In addition, at the site of the cuts on the

carcasses, there is evidence of high heat, over hundreds of degrees. This has been confirmed by microscopic evidence. Another remarkable fact about the mutilated corpses is that birds of prey and other predators leave them to rot naturally. Even flies and maggots are absent. Corpses are left facing east, with no footprints, wheel tracks or anything similar in the vicinity.

One theory suggests that the animals are being taken elsewhere for 'surgery' and, when brought back to the spot where they are found, are dropped from the air. This idea is supported by the broken bones found in the animals and sometimes snapped branches overhead. Authorities such as the FBI seem strangely disinterested in the phenomenon, dismissing the incidents as the work of predators, despite ranchers' experiences to the contrary. Researcher Chris O'Brien puts forward a possible explanation. Bio-tech companies are competing to find an artificial substitute for human blood, and the financial stakes in this are high. The haemoglobin found in the blood of cattle most closely resembles that of humans. Another theory is that deposits of metals like gold and silver can be detected by examining the tissue of cattle grazing nearby. The case may be similar for oil. Flying craft are usually seen over the mutilation sites, whether UFOs or unmarked helicopters. One rancher even reported seeing aliens carrying a cow towards the craft, and the animal was later found, mutilated. Another report described a beam of light from a spaceship drawing an animal up within it.

Although cattle are the most popular victims, horses, goats, sheep, pigs and even domestic pets have received this horrific treatment at the hands of the unknown surgeons. Whether aliens, unscrupulous scientists or some other agency are responsible, it is hard to understand the methods. Presumably cattle could be found more discreetly for research: instead of being taken from remote spots, animals are mutilated near urban areas and on small ranches. Researcher Jacques Vallée comments that this seems calculated to produce the maximum fear and alarm. However, an ex-Home Office contact of mine, whom I cannot name, states that although there are indeed several species of alien on earth at present, they do not carry out abductions, experiments or mutilations, and that these are the work of sinister human agencies. A chilling, mysterious matter.

CONSPIRACY

While you here do snoring lie
Open-eyed conspiracy
His time doth take:
If of life you keep a care
Shake off slumber and beware
Awake! Awake!

The Tempest, William Shakespeare (1564–1618)

You can fool some of the people all the time and all the people
some of the time, but you can't fool all the people all the time.

Abraham Lincoln (1809–1865)

For reasons of national security all governments naturally have their secrets. With war an ever-present possibility, no-one wants a potential aggressor to know all their military capability and other relevant information. And because it is quite impossible to swear a whole country to secrecy, much is withheld from the ordinary citizen. Besides, we all know politicians wilfully mislead us in order to get into power, and while we shake our heads about this, basically we accept it. We accept our position of ignorance and vulnerability, because we feel there is little we can do about it. But what if we are most ignorant and more vulnerable than we can imagine? In a climate of distrust and concealment, rumours fester. What if, besides being purposely misled, we are also being exploited? Rather than being treated like small children by a possibly misguided

but basically benign government, could we be a species of laboratory rat, offered up as part of a sinister bargaining system between our governments and alien visitors? This is the most extreme and bizarre scenario, held to be true by some UFO believers, who assert that the governments of the USA, Britain and some other countries have made a treaty with extra-terrestrials called the 'Greys', where advanced technology is swapped for permission to conduct experiments on humans and cattle. Such theories appeal to some, while others reject them as laughable. Let us look at the background.

The ORIGINS OF The THEORIES

During World War II there was much speculation concerning German technology and the development of advanced flying machines. Bomber pilots flying over enemy territory reported sighting balls of light near their wing-tips. These objects performed feats of aerial acrobatics. Strange figures were also seen aboard the planes, possibly originating, by some means unknown, from the balls of light. These light balls came to be called 'foo fighters' and the humanoids called 'gremlins' due to their disruption of sensitive equipment – this term has passed into popular terminology and describes a machine playing up. After the war it transpired that German pilots had also seen the strange balls of light. However, rumours persisted and still persist regarding sinister Nazi technology. The Soviets, too, were suspected of creating advanced flying machines with dangerous capabilities. Ghost rockets were reported, and a Nazi programme to build some unconventional saucer-shaped craft was believed by some to have been taken over by the US military. Speculation for this was fuelled by the Roswell incident (see Chapter 2). Another wreck occurred in the area of Aztec, New Mexico, on 25 March 1948 and rumours spread that a damaged saucer had been recovered with 16 alien bodies. Two and a half months earlier, and just six months after the Roswell incident, a Kentucky National Guard pilot was killed, in questionable circumstances.

Tommy Mantell was a decorated veteran of World War II, with over 2,800 hours of flight time chalked up. On the day in question he

was returning from Marietta, Georgia, with three other men in P-51 fighters. They received a call from Godman Field, Fort Knox, telling them to pursue an unidentified object that had been seen in the area. One of the aircraft did not comply because it was low on fuel, but Mantell and the other two continued. All the pilots reported seeing the object, but in due course Mantell's wing man turned back with the less experienced pilot, to escort him down – a fact which some experts find strange as a wing man is supposed to stay with the flight leader. Mantell radioed that he was going after a metallic object, doing half his speed. Mantell's last known words were: 'I see the object. I am going to pursue it a bit further.' He climbed to 33,000ft (10,000m) and is believed to have died from lack of oxygen while the aircraft continued to climb. The plane later crashed in a Kentucky field.

Mantell left a widow and two little boys. One of his sons, who was six at the time of his death, recalls how the Air Force did not tell his mother of his father's death. This was left to neighbours who told her that the plane had crashed. This son believes that there was a cover-up because no-one ever came to talk to them or to explain what had happened. Sensational stories in the media provoked the Air Force into suggesting that Mantell, the experienced veteran, died while pursuing a high-altitude balloon or the planet Venus! Due to the unusual wounds on the body he was buried in a closed casket. For his bereaved family, however, the matter was not, and never could be at an end. In the early 1990s a team from the programme 'Sightings' investigated further at the crash site, and succeeded in recovering some pieces of Mantell's plane that had been buried by the military. These pieces registered strong levels of radiation on a Geiger counter. There are those who believe that Mantell lost his life trying to protect his country from what he perceived to be a possible threat. Certainly there are many unanswered questions, such as why were bits of the downed plane, verifiable as Mantell's by the serial numbers, found buried in an unmarked spot by those who had promised to conduct a full investigation?

More controversy was unleashed by a certain Major Donald Keyhoe, a retired Major from the US Marine Corps. In *True* magazine (January, 1950) he stated that the Planet Earth was under surveillance by

extra-terrestrials and that this was known by top-level personnel in the armed forces, who were covering it up. His assertions were backed up by anonymous testimonies. In 1950 his book *The Flying Saucers Are Real* (Fawcett, 1950) was published and became a bestseller, and was quickly followed by *Aliens From Space* (Doubleday, 1973). While these works have been criticized for their poor documentation and lack of proof, they crystallized the rumours that were current. Through the 1940s and 1950s many sightings of unidentified craft were reported, including many from military personnel. The idea of aliens and government conspiracy took deep root in the minds of many, despite the absence of clear proof.

Project Blue Book

What vestiges of trust there remained in the general public for the establishment were demolished by the government investigation Project Blue Book, undertaken by the US Air Force from March 1952 to December 1969. This was a long and complex process in which hundreds of witnesses were questioned by highly-trained personnel. The final conclusion of this investigation was that there was no evidence for the existence of extra-terrestrials or their craft. However, much of the project's findings remain classified, and the public report issued was unconvincing.

Majestic 12

Majestic 12 was a government research team, designated classified. Information about this came into the public domain in 1982, when Bill Moore, a UFO researcher, and Jamie Shandera, a television producer, received a roll of film through the post. When developed, this revealed details of Operation Majestic, provided for President Eisenhower in 1952, detailing sightings of a craft, extra-terrestrial bodies recovered in the Roswell crash, a following crash in Texas and defining the decision of the investigators to keep the entire

matter top secret in order to avoid widespread panic, because the belief of the team was that the objects and bodies recovered did, in fact, originate from somewhere other than our planet.

A working group to investigate the Majestic 12 affair and the researchers Moore and Shandera was set up by the Defence Intelligence Agency, which in turn initiated an FBI investigation of the highest order. Getting nowhere with the Air Force, discounting fraud by the researchers and disinformation by foreign agencies, the FBI suggested that the working group might themselves have fabricated records of Project Majestic! What a tangled web we weave! As well as cover-up, misinformation and downright lying we also have 'disinformation' which is the purposeful 'leaking' of misleading information, presumably to detract attention from something else that is really going on. How convenient to send the media and researchers on a wild goose chase after flying saucers and aliens, so that no-one bothers too much to investigate other possibilities such as the development of advanced missiles, biological warfare devices and similar. Disinformation can also serve to discredit genuine witnesses by creating a sensationalist atmosphere.

Following the breaking of the Majestic story, former US Navy officer Bill Cooper went public confirming the account, and went even further, drawing on other top-secret sources to confirm the existence of photographs of aliens, US government departments designed to recover alien craft and test-fly them, and then to cover all traces of their activities. Agreement also exists whereby aliens are permitted to examine cattle and humans for their research, returning the human unharmed and informing the government agency responsible for keeping track of them. In return for this alien technology was given, but the aliens, the afore mentioned Greys, have broken the terms of the agreement, abducting humans and mutilating cattle. In addition the aliens have placed implants in the brains of their subjects, so they can monitor and control them. The estimate given in the government reports attached to Majestic was of one in forty Americans having been given implants by alien abductors! The US government, according to Cooper, is alarmed by the fact it has so little effective control over the aliens and fears also that if the news were to become public mass hysteria would ensue. However, Majestic is

now regarded as almost definitely a hoax by most UFO researchers, one of the reasons being that the so-called government documents involved do not conform to the usual system of numbering.

Area 51

Also known as Groom Lake, and 'Dreamland', this famed 'secret' base in Nevada is implicated in stories of captive aliens, mysterious tests and experiments, and immortalized in the film *Independence Day* as holding sinister, preserved aliens and their craft, without even the President knowing! Cooper confirmed that this Base was used to test-fly captured alien craft. Groom Lake Base is part of the Nevada Nuclear Test Site and the home of many top-secret projects such as Stealth and SDI. To those who believe whole-heartedly in conspiracy, this site is the epicentre of whole sinister game.

Physicist Bob Lazar claims to have worked closely with aliens at Groom Lake, and to have studied methods of extra-terrestrial propulsion that manipulate gravity. Lazar's claims of having worked for Naval Intelligence have been verified.

Tales about secret bases where humans work with aliens on advanced technology do not stop with Area 51, but extend to rumours about a vast network of underground tunnels connecting many US military and scientific bases, where extra-terrestrials can roam at will. This does not seem to have been substantiated, and is indeed one of the more far-fetched accounts, simply because the size of the engineering programme required to create these tunnels is inconceivable. Too many people would have to have been kept quiet for it to have remained as 'secret' as it has, in addition to the amount of money and upheaval involved. Unless, of course, the aliens did it with incomprehensible technology!

Whatever the truth may be about Groom Lake/Area 51 there is little doubt that something is going on there, with or without alien help. As recently as 1995 the US government denied its existence. The presence of a smokescreen is an irresistible invitation to the imagination to run wild. Truth, however, is often stranger than fiction.

The Men in Black

The most sinister figures of UFO folklore are the Men in Black (MIBs), whose appearance would seem, on the face of it, to confirm the idea of government 'cover up'. The MIBs wear black suits and dark glasses, riding in brand new black Cadillacs. Often they have a faintly Oriental air, dark skin and an artificial way of expressing themselves. Characteristically, they approach those who have witnessed a UFO or a related incident and warn them against saying anything to anyone, sometimes threatening them. Often they seem to know all about the life of the person concerned and may appear on the scene even before the shocked witness has had a chance to tell anyone else about the encounter. Many highly credible people have reported contact with these men, from vastly different backgrounds and circumstances. Accounts of the MIBs are so widespread and convincing that there seems little doubt that something is going on.

The menacing figures of the Men in Black in UFO folklore are reported to play a part in the cover-ups of UFO and alien encounters.

Some people say that the MIBs are in fact aliens, others that they are government agents. The mystery of the MIBs remains one of the more inexplicable facets of the entire UFO phenomenon.

The conspiracy theory evaluated

Could it be possible for major governments throughout the world to be in league with aliens and to have kept and be keeping this knowledge from the general public? To assess the question we need to think about the actualities of government and the amount of people involved and the unwieldy nature of bureaucracy. Logically, it does not seem possible that a complex conspiracy of this sort, involving large numbers of people could possibly have been kept under wraps. For this reason we can probably dismiss tales of tunnel networks and similar, because there would have been too many people involved in carrying out such a project, at least from the knowledge we have, excluding speculation about ray guns and such like.

However, there are several points that do indeed support at least the vivid possibility that such a conspiracy, or something similar does exist. In the first place, we know that governments don't tell their people the truth. They do not even pretend to, with such labels as 'Top Secret' and 'Classified' attached to certain matters. For reasons of national security? No doubt, but what if they were misapplied, for cynical reasons?

Secondly, in such a conspiracy, how many people would actually need to know all the facts? Conceivably, total knowledge of the operation could be the privilege of a mere handful. The fact that there have, as it happens, been a large number of 'leaks' could be taken as proof that you cannot, indeed, keep such a conspiracy completely silent. Which leads to point three, no-one really wants to believe that we are being experimented upon by little green men. Most of us want our little world and reality-as-we-know-it to remain intact, and if this were true – I mean *really true* – where does that

leave us as humans? A whole new perspective would be drawn on the work-home-pub-and-shopping fabric of most people's lives.

The last, and in a way most sinister, point concerns the capabilities of humans themselves. We do not find it hard to accept that occasionally leaders come to positions of influence who are cynical, power-hungry and utterly callous. However, we and our friends and the guy or gal next door are quite different. We would never intentionally hurt someone. Sadly, in scientific research quite the opposite is the case. Most of us, faced with a situation where we are told to do something by a person in 'authority', backed up by official sanction, do it, even if it means causing observable harm to another. To prove this, tests were carried out on a variety of subjects. They were told that it was their job to press a button that would cause severe pain to someone in an adjoining room, that this person had agreed to be part of this, and that it was all part of an important scientific experiment. Despite screams of agony emanating from behind the partition, again and again the subject pressed the button, reluctantly, it is true, in many cases, but nevertheless obeying the request. Faced with blandishments, assurances and higher authority most of us would do the same. This is not to say that ordinary people in considerable numbers are acquiescing to and actively supporting experiments by aliens on their compatriots, but rather that in a hierarchical structure people do not ask questions. They are even more unlikely to ask questions if there have been subtle or overt threats against them, their families, reputations or livelihood.

None of these considerations means anything concrete. There is no 'proof' that aliens have landed, let alone that they are using the earth as a vast test-tube. It is merely a word to the wise on how easily we may be misled, or mislead ourselves. Possibilities cover a wide spectrum, from alien conspiracy down to government disingenuity of one kind or another related in some way to the profits of large companies who are backing the said government. In such cases, it is much better for the public to be in a flap about aliens than examining their cereal packets for the listing of GMO ingredients. What is clear, however, is that *something*, in fact a great deal, *is being covered up*. How significant this may be we cannot know at present. For proof of a cover-up, on a small but interesting

scale, I turn now to information supplied to me by Robin Cole, of the Circular Forum in Cheltenham.

Intelligence agencies

In Britain we have essentially three intelligence services that form the central intelligence 'machinery'. These include MI5, the Security Service and MI6, the Secret Intelligence Service. These are familiar to anyone who is interested in crime and spy television programmes (or who has them inflicted upon them!). The third agency, Government Communications Headquarters, known as GCHQ is the 'hub of all intelligence operations throughout the UK' providing information for MI5 and MI6 in addition to other government departments, including the Ministry of Defence. Despite the ending of the Cold War, GCHQ continues to grow and its unattractive edifices, which require no planning permission, strike a note of discord with the graceful buildings of Cheltenham Spa, Gloucestershire. More than 5,000 people are employed here and they are vetted thoroughly, down to their sexual proclivities, hobbies and family backgrounds. I even know of one person whose hairdresser was questioned, presumably due to the possibility that she was not a 'natural' blonde!

No matter how mundane the post, the Official Secrets Act must be signed by all employees. The work cannot be discussed with anyone outside, so not even the families of employees have any idea what they do at work. Not surprisingly this causes considerable stress, and as a counsellor I am aware that more than a few people from GCHQ are driven to seek marital or personal therapy at some time. However, even during therapy they cannot discuss any aspects of their work that may be causing them concern – or even admit they are concerned. Compared to other types of employment, the suicide rate is high. Work is compartmentalized, working on a need to know basis, so no-one is in possession of more information that is absolutely necessary. Employees who inform on the indiscretions of their colleagues are liable to be promoted more quickly, achieve higher pay, etc. This results in a rather paranoid atmosphere, and I am reminded of the phrase 'Where there's fear there's power'. It

seems to me that the 'power' here resides at the top of the organization with the people who hold the purse strings and have the ability to hire and fire. Is an organization like this essential to national security? Possibly, but it seems to me that it is liable to misuse.

According to Cole this is 'probably one of the most secure places in Britain. Even when you telephone them a simple 'Hello' is all you will get.' High-security fences, topped with razor wire, protect the two establishments that comprise GCHQ, along with check points, state-of-the-art camera and CCTV. Guns are available in case of terrorist attack.

The function of GCHQ is to gather intelligence and develop technology, in many ways and covering many aspects. Most people are aware of Sigint (Signal Intelligence), where the various departments are given information covertly acquired. This includes downloading signals from satellites and anything that comes their way. Because of this it controls the Composite Signals Organization, operating in the UK and abroad. On a more mundane level, the world's press is sifted through, for relevant information. Not surprisingly, the technology here is advanced, with 'Super Computers' being continually upgraded. Millions of words can be monitored within seconds, with certain keywords alerting the computers to information which may be relevant, in which case the conversation is recorded and printed. All foreign calls are monitored and some domestic ones, including fax, telex and e-mail. The only areas that cause problems are Internet and digital encryption – for now. The technology exists to replicate a person's voice, so with bugging and micro-chips any situation can be controlled, as long as the person whose voice is being replicated is safely absent! There are also links with the National Criminal Intelligence Service, enabling possible mail-tampering, bugging and surveillance technology for anything or anyone suspect. In addition, GCHQ is responsible for official and military communications, knows about military aircraft worldwide, monitors satellites, and develops new techniques of 'mind warfare' and propaganda. Besides this, it provides banks and stock exchanges with advice on computer security.

The technology that resides here is mind-blowing. GCHQ is not covered by the Data Protection Act, enabling them to store

information of any kind on anyone or anything. GCHQ matches the US National Security Agency, and the annual budget for the two sites is £500 million.

Most significantly, GCHQ plays an official role as advisor to the government during certain situations that are based on the intelligence information obtained and how to control the outcome. This is a role they have played in the past, and the part they played in the incident we shall be discussing. We need to understand the function of the organization to understand the relevance, for GCHQ may have some answers of interest to ufologists.

Incident in the Wash

At 3.14 a.m. on 5 October 1996 Mr Leyland of Skegness Police telephoned Yarmouth Coastguards reporting an object spotted airborne over the sea, by numerous police officers: 'We can see a strange red and green rotating light in the sky directly southeast from Skegness. Looks to be high in the sky over the Wash,' runs the full incident report. This was the start of a major incident involving not only the local police but also the crew of the Conocoast shipping tanker, civil aircraft, RAF Neatishead, RAF Kinloss, RAF Northwood, RAF Waddington, Anglia Radar, Claxby Radar, London Northwood Radar, the MOD, Whitehall and, of course, GCHQ. Because of the number of people involved, Cole has had to sift through a great deal of complex information.

The incident report was certainly a reliable and accurate record of what had been observed and what had occurred. As is normal procedure, the Coastguards entered developments on to the computer as they arose. All incoming and outgoing telephone conversations are routinely taped by the Coastguards offices. Radar contact was also made with the said object. Whatever this may have been it had no transponder, which all aircraft are required to have, and so it could not be identified. Suspecting a drugs run they tried to coax the Customs and Excise aircraft to intercept the object, but this was engaged elsewhere. Attempts to contact Special Branch at

Norwich obtained only an answer phone. In the opinion of Customs and Excise a drugs run was unlikely because a guilty helicopter would hardly stay, hovering, and RAF Kinloss confirmed that this would not have been possible for a helicopter as the object was there for several hours and a helicopter would have been past its endurance by this time.

The full incident report now recounts that RAF Neatishead tried to run a trace on the object. RAF Kinloss phoned the Coastguards on their behalf with the words 'cannot explain it'. The crew of the Conocoast could see an object and so did a civilian plane, who reported the sighting to RAF Northwood. Aware of events, they passed the report to RAF Neatishead. Police at Skegness, at the request of the Coastguards, videoed the object from the top of their station. A copy of this tape is now in the possession of Cole.

In the interest of objectivity, Cole points out that because of the numbers of people involved it is quite possible that some people observed a celestial body and that some radar returns were due to clutter caused by increased sensitivity, as the RAF stations increased the output to locate the object. This would explain some of the discrepancies. However, this is a highly notable and verified UFO incident. As such, it is, of course, one of many such happenings. For our purposes here, what is of greatest interest is the way the authorities choose to handle such matters.

The official line

Cole writes:

> As soon as the story hit the press, the MOD were telling everyone it was Venus, weather phenomena and Boston Stump – a church tower inland from the coast which accounted for the radar contacts. However, Nigel Sergeant (an MOD spokesperson) prior to the main press coverage had stated to a reporter from one of the local tabloids that 'We are trying to prove (emphasis Robin's) that it does not represent any sort of security threat and that it was not an aggressive intrusion into our airspace'. An inadvertent slip of the tongue or a very naive Government official?

If we unpack the information, we find that Venus, as confirmed by the Greenwich Royal Observatory, broke the horizon at 3.10 a.m. and would not have been clearly visible for another 8 to 10 minutes. Mr Leyland's report to the Coastguards was timed 3.14 a.m. describing the object as 'high in the sky'. Besides this, police officers (and there were many involved) had already been observing the object for some time before making the report. 'One of the most important parts of police training is the observation and assessment of a situation prior to any action,' writes Cole. I would further say that any policeman who could describe Venus as a 'strange red and green rotating light' is not one I would wish to consult about a lost handbag!

Regarding Boston Stump, the supposed culprit of the radar confusion, this church tower has been standing at a height of 272ft (81.6m) for over 100 years. If radar could have picked it up they would already have known it was there. It does seem to me that if a church tower can confuse radar to that extent our national defence isn't worth much.

Regarding the supposed 'storm', the police and crew of the Conocoast stated there was no storm in the Wash that morning. The full incident report says the sky was clear, with a wind of 12 knots and a slight swell on the sea. Visibility was 20 miles (32km). No known object could retain a completely stationery position in the sky for several hours, with that wind speed. The Coastguards told Cole that they had been told to give these explanations from 'higher up', and they believed this was the MOD.

Cole had a chance meeting with an acquaintance who has a close association with GCHQ. He laughingly asked if he was still interested in 'all that UFO stuff' and when he received an affirmative reply, asked: 'What's been going on in East Anglia then?' At that time Cole had little knowledge of the incident, having been out of the country at the time. In any case, it is not considered good practice for UFO researchers to investigate cases outside their own county, as these are the province of the local UFO experts. Cole said he was unsure, and asked why? His acquaintance then told him that during the night of the incident senior civil servants had been called in to GCHQ.

More information needed to be teased out of Cole's informant over several more meetings. This acquaintance, whose identity has been

protected for obvious reasons, asked that the information be kept confidential – an undertaking to which Cole decided not to adhere, in the interests of public awareness, and also to show how seriously such phenomena are in truth regarded by those in power, and how often the public and ufologists are deceived, or intended to be deceived, by misleading statements.

Naturally, the story of what happened in the Wash was widely reported in UFO magazines. Subsequent to the event, the Labour MP for Don Valley, Mr Martin Redmond, tabled some questions in the Commons about the UFO, addressed to both the Prime Minister and the Secretary of State. The Rt. Hon David Davis MP, Minister of State for Foreign and Commonwealth Affairs, was asked if he would 'list by month for each of the last ten years and this year (1996) to date the number of occasions on which the Government Communications Headquarters has monitored unidentified flying object investigations' and to make a statement on the matter. Mr Davies replied that he would write to the Honourable Member shortly. Sadly, Mr Redmond died from cancer before he could reply to Cole's query regarding the outcome, and although his secretary agreed to try to find the details, nothing arrived.

Cole also wrote to the Director of GCHQ, Mr David Omand requesting information on past and present government UFO-related activity. The reply he received was interesting, stating that:

> …we would not normally reply to a letter of this kind, given it is our firm policy not to comment on intelligence operations. In this case however I would not want to leave you with any impression that we are concealing work on UFOs. We are not engaged in any way whatsoever in any monitoring for suspected UFOs, and we hold no information from our normal work which would shed any light on the debate whether UFOs have or have not ever been detected.'

Note that the statement concerns 'monitoring' not simply any tasks. Cole's investigations have revealed, as we saw, that GCHQ was involved in the October 1996 incident, and that this was not the first time. Their 'normal' work involves policing air space and they would not have 'normally' replied: something doesn't smell quite right.

On 3 January 1997, Cole sent a third letter to Kerry Philpott at Air Staff Secretariat, MOD Whitehall, the official co-ordination point for UFO matters (commonly called 'the UFO Desk'). One of the questions in the latter concerned the involvement and role of GCHQ in all reports that do not have down-to-earth explanations. The upshot of the reply was that Philpott was not prepared to comment. Her predecessor, Nick Pope (author of *Open Skies, Closed Minds*, Simon and Schuster, 1996) was also approached. He states that it was government policy not to comment on the operations of the intelligence and security agencies and that this was the line he was taking, with the parting shot: 'I am sure you will appreciate that this can be my only response on such matters.' As Cole says, if they are simply not involved, why not say so? Perhaps because after several leaks a denial would not be believed. Further questions to the MOD have received similar evasive replies. Cole is still waiting to hear from Mr Davis, the MP questioned in the Commons by Mr Redmond. He can, however, confirm that on 7 October 1996 a Wing Commander at Whitehall was still requesting a large amount of information about the events and the sighting in the Wash, including maps and the current location of the video footage taken.

GCHQ and UFOs

The following section is taken almost verbatim from Cole's self-published booklet:

A look at some of GCHQ's previous involvement in the UFO phenomenon had also prompted me to publish this document. It is now becoming abundantly clear that they do, to some extent and intermittently, when a threat does occur (despite MOD claims that they don't) take UFO sightings extremely seriously.

The earliest event that I can link them to is in or around June 1952. This came to me as 'off the record' information from an informant who was told of events at the time. Pilots from what used to be RAF Little Rissington were out on manoeuvres when an object, similar to the descriptions of a flying saucer, came into

view. *Receiving permission to go after the object, they then kept in constant contact with the RAF base. Radar control had the object on screen, and heading towards Cornwall they pursued it.*

At this point one aircraft returned (the reason is unclear) whilst the other continued. On reaching the coast the unidentified object put on tremendous speed leaving the ... aircraft well behind. This was also noted on radar. Realizing he had no chance of catching the object up the pilot simply returned and was debriefed accordingly. GCHQ were fully aware of the event.

Much more recently, on the 29 March 1996, two security guards at GCHQ observed two large bright objects directly above the Oakley site that they were protecting. The objects appeared just after 4.20 a.m. and flew at incredible speed and in complete silence. The guards approached the local paper who ran their story in a small article several pages in.

Since the first flying saucer reports of the 1950s, government bodies worldwide have taken the issue more seriously than we may have previously believed.

The guards were called before their superiors and told not to mention it again, and that they had not seen anything. They were told that what they had seen, should anyone ask, was the Space Station Mir and Space Shuttle Columbia docking. The reason, I am told, for this dressing down, was for security reasons. By having their names published they could open themselves up to blackmail and extortion. Considering the amount of people who work at the two sites (of GCHQ) and who have also had their names in the local press with regards to their hobbies or charity events, it seems odd that none of them are aware of this reporting restriction.

A phone call to the United States and NASA's Records Office soon established that the Mir and Columbia were not even visible from England during that week. Both were orbiting over the furthest reaches of the South Atlantic. Given the size of the objects seen by the guards it would also mean that these space stations were well down within our own atmosphere. This doesn't mean however, that another mundane explanation isn't possible.

Without actually speaking with the guards concerned (despite attempts) it is difficult to substantiate fully the events that occurred, and therefore I am unable to pass further comment.

Another interesting thought concerns GCHQ's library, which contains a number of books relating to the UFO phenomenon, and which contains an artificial copy of Project Blue Book [mentioned earlier in this chapter].

One source, who has or did have [Cole is not prepared to state which] links with the radar facilities at the Benhall site, confirmed after much cajolery that yes, they do occasionally track objects which have no explanation and which perform incredible feats. When pushed for an explanation the person simply stated they knew of no technology that even slightly resembled the characteristics of these unidentified objects, but did state that they [i.e. those within GCHQ] thought of them privately as being an alien technology. For them, it brightened up the course of a day's work when a UFO did appear...

I have it on extremely good authority that on the night in question [i.e. the incident in the Wash] at least two senior civil servants (whose names I have been passed) received a telephone call in their homes in the early hours of 5 October, as the events were unfolding. They were requested to report to the Oakle Site. On arrival they were briefed on the situation and the incursion into UK air space ... Their conclusion was that the event involved an Unidentified Flying Object, and that it was advised the 'usual' lines of enquiry be made, what the implications were, how best to play the incident down and what further course of action should be taken. This included how best to brief the government!...

What the media and public do not get to see is the amount of official documentation concerning these objects, unless of course they spend a great deal of time rooting around following up leads, visiting the Public Records Office, making applications under the American Freedom Of Information Act and generally spending a lot of time and money on the subject...

Cole also has two copies of UFO reports from the Civil Aviation Authorities safety regulation group at Gatwick Airport. One report tells of a sighting of a large translucent object, approx 500ft (150m) long, observed at 4,100ft (1,250m) by all on board the aircraft. The date given is 12 June 1982, location Dinkelsbuhi, Operator Dan-Air, B727, Occnum 8201614C. The second described how a Kondair Trislander struck an object while flying, damaging the fusilage, propellor and other parts of the aircraft. Three pieces of a foreign metallic object were found after an emergency landing, including a small cylindrical magnet. The date was 24 August 1984, the location Ipswich.

In addition, as we know, there are countless well-documented reports from pilots and other professionals of good standing. The accounts given above are not remarkable for their content, and are naturally weakened, as is always the case with such material, by the fact that not all the sources can be named. In this way pressure, intimidation and denial contaminate even what is available for scrutiny. Is this a healthy atmosphere?

Conclusion

We are not left in a place of any certainty by this patiently assembled data, at least not regarding the nature of UFOs and whether we are really being regularly visited by extra-terrestrials in super spacecraft. However, if we are to believe Cole and his anonymous informants (and I would personally vouch for the fact that Cole is a patient and thorough seeker after truth, not a sensationalist fabricator) then we do know that *something* is being kept from us by an extremely powerful and technologically advanced government agency. Furthermore, despite its super-computers, its enormous budget, its hundreds of highly trained personnel and its ultra-advanced technology, perhaps GCHQ does not understand the meaning and nature of the events that it is studying – and shrouding. The questions continue…

Practice

I asked Robin Cole what advice he would give to anyone wishing to investigate conspiracy and cover-up in relation to UFOs. His advice was to start with a reputable magazine, such as *UFO*. Find out about local groups, and, if you are truly of the bloodhound mentality, you will soon pick up a scent that interests you. This can be an expensive and time-consuming process.

Cole himself is very pleased to receive calls and letters and has authorized me to give out his telephone number and contact address, which you will find at the back of the book. He will treat all enquiries and information in complete confidence, and will be especially pleased to hear from anyone who has links with any of the government agencies or departments mentioned, or who knows anyone else who has, and who possesses information that cannot be imparted due to restrictions. Cole feels strongly that until information about the UFO phenomenon is made freely and openly available for proper scrutiny by all interested and informed parrties, we will not be able to come to any conclusions. The truth is out there.

I can trace my ancestry back to a protoplasmal atomic globule.

Sir W.S. Gilbert, *The Mikado* 1885

In the chapter on the Philadelphia Experiment we saw that Dr Morris Jessup was one of the first known proponents of the Ancient Astronaut Theory. This theory has a variety of forms, but it basically suggests that aliens have been on our earth before, not as an ambiguous phenomenon in the sky, but actively, and in considerable numbers, having an effect upon our history and development. Speculation that these advanced beings were behind the construction of the pyramids and other technologically baffling structures is not uncommon. A factor that also suggests possible early extra-terrestrial visits is the sophisticated astronomical knowledge possessed by many ancient cultures. Further, linguistic tracing reveals a common root to ancient languages, hinting at a once universal civilization. *Homo sapiens* appeared very suddenly, not, in fact, over millennia as suggested by evolutionary theory. In addition, ancient texts describe many encounters with the gods, and while these are dismissed by scholars as myths, reports about wars and harvests, appearing alongside, are taken literally.

Charles Fort, whom we met in Chapter 1 as the originator of the term 'Fortean Phenomena', subscribed to the ancient astronaut idea. There are many archeological enigmas that do not fit our beliefs about the progress of history. These include electric batteries made many millennia in the past, optical lenses of a similar age, wrought iron found embedded in unmined coalfaces, vases with necks so

thin we could not reproduce them today, and many others. High resolution photography from space now reveals enormous artificial earthworks previously unnoticed and sophisticated canal systems in Florida and Mesopotamia dating from prehistory. On the basis of all these and other anomalies, alien intervention has been postulated. Some writers go so far as to say that human beings were genetically engineered, specially bred, or even created by aliens, who may have been our ancestors, donating their genetic material to make seedling *Homo sapiens*. As far as I am aware, none of these theories has ever been proven, and most have been greeted with intellectual scorn. However, none have been disproved either. Of course, it is not pleasing to the human ego to contemplate the possibility that we are not Galactic Top Species. Nonetheless, from a perspective of light years distant, the possibility that our planet was colonized, thousands of years ago, by an advanced alien race, seems perfectly reasonable.

Erich von Daniken

The writer who is known most of all for publicizing the idea of prehistoric alien visitation is Erich von Daniken. In his books *Chariots of the Gods* and *The Gold of the Gods* (see Further reading) he made literal interpretations of Biblical texts, where the 'Elohim' breed with the 'daughters of man': von Daniken took this to mean beings from other worlds landed and begat our forbears. He also seized upon many physical relics, to support his theories.

Old maps exist, called 'portolans' that scholars discount as being flawed by poor medieval map-making technology: study of these maps reveals that their standard of accuracy actually decreased as time went by, and fresh copies were made of older material. The most well-known of these maps is that of the Turkish sailor Piri Re'is. One of the most interesting points about his map is that the contours of Antarctica are displayed. Von Daniken and others believe that the only way the Antarctic shoreline could have been mapped was by aerial observation – something that would only have been available to primitive people through the agency of

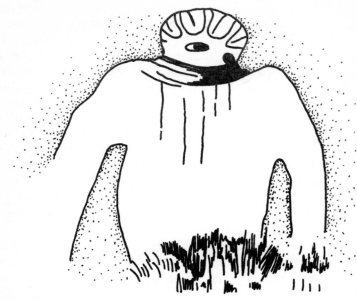

Ancient rock carvings have been interpreted by some researchers as being evidence of ancient alien visitors.

visiting aliens. However, there are other scholars who make a good case for the existence of an advanced terrestrial civilization, before Antarctica was covered with ice, who were swept away by a huge cataclysm possibly involving a pole shift, a collision with a meteor or something similar. It is argued that vestiges of their technology may be found in such works as the pyramids.

Von Daniken interpreted many rock carvings, paintings and artefacts as evidence of alien visits. In Val Camonica in Italy a prehistoric carving shows a figure wearing antlers, which von Daniken described as 'antennae'. Of course, horns were often worn by nature-worshipping people as a way of identifying with their gods, and, indeed, of entering into a mystical communion with animals that were to be their prey. Even today some pagans wear a crown of horns on occasion, in honour of the Horned God (this has nothing to do with 'devil-worship' but is a way of honouring our roots and the power of

Nature). The 'antennae' theory seems far-fetched, for why should ancient astronauts have worn antennae anyway, unless we presuppose a technology rather like our own, in which case they would hardly have got here in the first place! However, the figure depicted in the drawings is possibly ambiguous, although there exist perfectly legitimate, tribal explanations. Similarly the rock paintings of Tassili in the Sahara show figures with 'antennae' that are more probably hallucinogenic mushrooms, used to induce trance states. One of the Tassilli figures looks like a one-eyed humanoid with flattened banana-skins on its forehead. Archaeologists called this figure the 'Martian', which von Daniken was quick to seize upon.

The lines on the Nazca pampa, in Peru, were some of von Daniken's best 'evidence'. These straight line features are indeed fascinating, having been constructed two millennia ago by removing the surface desert rock to the level of the lighter soil below. Some of the lines are simply narrow pathways, while some markings are much larger. One theory now suggests these lines were made by shamanic peoples as a representation of the out-of-body journey of the soul, and thus linked to straight line features worldwide, also called ley lines (see Chapter 7 and *Earth Mysteries: a Beginner's Guide* and *Ley Lines: a Beginner's Guide* also in this series). Von Daniken saw the Nazca lines as a sort of 'space-port'. More subtly, the earth energy believed by many people to run along ley lines has been described by certain theorists as terrestrial forces made use of by UFO crews. UFOs (along with other strange phenomena) are more often seen in areas where this earth force is felt to be strongest. In regard to the Nazca lines, it must be remembered that the desert is easily marked, and if von Daniken's ancient astronauts flew craft with propulsion systems akin to anything with which we are familiar, they would surely have left their own indelible mark in the rainless desert. No such marks exist.

The idea of UFOs and the 'earth force' was put forward by an ex-RAF pilot, Tony Wedd, in the 1960s and, along with allied subjects has been explored by John Michell in *The Flying Saucer Vision* (Sidgwick & Jackson, 1967), and in *The View Over Atlantis* (Abacus, 1968). Von Daniken's vision was, and is far simpler and much more literal. They came, we saw them, interacted with them and left artefacts to later generations to prove it. Ancient spirituality gives way to ancient

spacemen: even the Egyptian *ka* soul becomes an aircraft, and Stonehenge a flying saucer. Von Daniken's work has many inaccuracies, and his lack of solid research has earned him the scorn of many serious thinkers. This may be a shame, because it has shuffled the entire Ancient Astronaut Theory into the backstreets of the weird-and-wonderful, when perhaps we should consider it more seriously.

Zachariah Sitchin

Stories in the Bible, when not subject to the bias of the translator, may contain some interesting and puzzling information. For instance, Ezekial's fiery chariot checks out aerodynamically as a possible shuttlecraft. Bible scholar and translator Zachariah Sitchin was especially impressed however, by the Sumerian people who established a civilization in Sumer in the fourth millennium BC. The Sumerians believed that all they did was through the grace of the gods, and they may have meant this literally. Their texts state that these 'gods' or beings lived among them within the temple, and each controlled a particular city, although they made visits to each other. Other gods lived in the skies. Those that came down to earth did so in 'whirlwinds' and 'divine birds' that remained on the top of their temples. Sumerian drawings depict these as rocket-type shapes that give out flames, or round objects.

One of the oldest Sumerian texts, the *Enuma Elish,* tells of the formation of the great gods out of the galactic gases, which were the sun and the planets. There was a battle between two of the planets, Marduk (also called Nibiru) and the enormous planet Tiamat. The Sumerians were remarkably accurate concerning the constitution of the outer planets, now confirmed by Voyager. Sumerian drawings depict our solar system accurately, with the addition of Tiamat orbiting in what is now the asteroid belt, between Mars and Jupiter, and Marduk. Marduk, according to the texts, came from outside the solar system, entrapped by the sun's gravity, and now has an elliptical orbit that takes it far out into space, and then back, close to earth every 3,600 years. On one of its entries into our solar system

Marduk crashed into Tiamat, breaking it up into the asteroids and into a ball of rock that became our earth. This new planet earth was seeded with genetic material from Marduk. To the Sumerians, Marduk was the home of the gods.

Around 450,000 years ago, according to the Sumerians, the 'Anunnaki' – the 'gods' on Marduk – came to earth to look for gold. According to Sitchin this was to strengthen the atmosphere of the planet by suspending particles of gold in it, for the internal heating system of Marduk had begun to become a threat. Some of the Sumerian beliefs are supported by science. For instance, there may well be several bodies orbiting the sun in an ellipse, and a body located in the direction of Orion by the Infa-Red Astronomical Observatory could indeed be the tenth planet. Pluto, believed by the Sumerians to have been a moon of Saturn, was displaced by Marduk on one of its visits, and this concurs with the opinions of some astronomers, who point out that it is too small to be so far from the sun. In addition, a theory has been put forward that the earth was indeed 'seeded' by tiny organisms from another planet and this has achieved scientific acclaim.

Sitchin details many Sumerian records of the Anunnaki, who left 'watchers' overhead while the landing party descended to earth, splashing down in the Indian Ocean and building a landing base in the Sinai. Then they began mining gold in Africa, where unbelievably ancient mines have in fact been discovered. The mining was hard graft, and the rank and file held the commander Enlil hostage, until his brother Enki placed the image of gods upon a lowly creature, probably *Homo erectus*. In other words the Anunnaki mixed their genetic material with the indigenous earthlings. These hybrids were, according to Sitchin, sterile, like mules, but Enki gave them the ability to reproduce. This scenario may be behind the story of the Garden of Eden, which is often interpreted as being sexual. In this version Enki is the serpent who gave us the forbidden fruit of sexual know-how. However, the rest of the Anunnaki were less than pleased and the new race were thrown out of the comfort of their protection (the equivalent of the expulsion from Eden). They spread across the world, first of all to Sumer, Egypt and the Indus Valley, where the earliest signs of civilization have actually been found.

A difficult situation rose as interbreeding occurred between the 'gods' and humans. Enlil cast about for a remedy, which materialized in the form of the return of Marduk, which, the Anunnaki knew, would cause the polar ice caps to shift and melt, due to the pull of its gravity. This would drown the beings left on the planet. However, Enki, who loved his creation, told Utnapishtim (the equivalent of Noah) what was going to happen. The ark was built, the gods departed to safety, the flood arrived. Afterwards it was found that humanity had survived, and they were used to build bases for the gods, and later their own cities.

The rivalry between Enki and Enlil was passed on to their descendents, and humans were used like pieces on a chessboard by the warring factions. Nuclear bombs destroyed Sodom and Gomorrah and the spaceport in Sinai (where satellite photography has located a large, blackened scar on the surface of our planet, that scientists cannot explain.) The waters of the Dead Sea, where Sodom and Gomorrah are believed to have been, are radioactive. From there a radioactive cloud drifted towards Sumer and decimated the population, reflected in the 'lamentation texts' of the cities of Sumer. This end to a Golden Age is recounted in many ancient texts, for at this point the gods withdrew in horror. These events are paralleled in ancient Hindu accounts, of gods who travelled in 'flying machines' or *vimanas*.

While Sitchin's interpretations are indeed subjective, they are based on available texts. It seems to me that until we truly understand the mind set of the people who wrote those texts, any interpretation must be 'subjective', including those of orthodox science and religion. However one looks at the matter, the Sumerians arose from the Stone Age in the space of three generations and their advanced knowledge of astronomy has been proved. What else, dismissed as fantasy, is destined to become fact?

The Sirius Mystery

The Sirius Mystery is the title of a book, by Robert Temple (see Further reading) in which he gives detailed evidence taken from

Egyptian, Greek and other texts, of alien visitation to our planet. These classical sources drew, Temple demonstrates, from the same tradition as the Dogon, whose revelations are more specific.

The Dogon live in the present state of Mali, close to Timbuctu. Temple demonstrates that ancient peoples privy to the tradition of Sirius migrated from Greece and Libya through the Sahara to the region of the Dogon, where they interbred with the indigenous natives, eventually mingling with them, but retaining their special traditions as a secret doctrine – which indeed was how the Dogon regarded their Sirian knowledge, until anthropologist Marcel Griaule earned their respect to the extent they decided to communicate it to him.

The Dogon consider Sirius B to be the most important star in the heavens. Sirius A is a very bright star, close to us, but Sirius B, its tiny companion, cannot be seen with the naked eye, yet the Dogon knew of it, and evidently have done for many centuries. In addition, they knew, without the help of the astronomer Kepler, who discovered that the planets orbit our sun in elliptical paths, that Sirius B orbits Sirius A in an ellipse, of which Sirius A is one of the foci (an ellipse, in contrast to a circle, has two foci, not one focus, or centre). They also knew that the time taken by Sirius B to complete an orbit is fifty of our years, and that it rotates on its own axis. They believe this rotational period to be the equivalent of one year, and they honour this in the 'bado' rite, when rays carrying special signals are beamed towards earth. These two beliefs have not been verified by science, but another has – the fact that the Dogon say that Sirius B is the smallest star, it is also the heaviest. Sirius B is in fact a white dwarf, made of incredibly dense material. The Dogon also speak of a third star in the Sirius system, with the same orbital period but a greater trajectory, this body being four times as light as Sirius B. The existence of Sirius C was, in fact, confirmed by astronomers in 1995. Dogon tradition also contains many facts about our solar system now verified by astronomers. They also knew about the turning of the earth on its axis, conceived of life on other planets and, incidentally, knew about the circulation of the blood.

From Sirius, according to the Dogon, came Nommo, an amphibious creature, much wiser than the peoples of the earth who come to 'save' them. Nommo destroyed what was brutish in human beings.

According to the Dogon, Nommo dies as a sacrifice for humanity and resurrects, so cleansing the earth. Similarities with the story of Christ are remarkable, even to the point of the crucifixion of Nommo, upon a tree. Nommo, according to the Dogon, will return on the Day of the Fish, and on this day a new star will be seen in the sky as the first indication. Then they will land, in their 'Ark' which will emit fire and great noise, and they will rule from the waters.

Temple traces many links within the mythology and culture of the Egyptians, Greeks, and Babylonians to elements of the Sirius lore. For instance, the number 50 features in many myths, linked notably with the mythical ship, the Argo. The mysteries of Isis, Nephthys, Anubis, Osiris and others of the Egyptian pantheon also fit, and there are endless associations and parallels, especially etymologically. It may be hard to imagine why knowledge about Sirius was encoded in myths in quite so obscure a fashion, but then we do not understand what we arrogantly call the 'primitive' mind set, and truthfully do not understand the meanings of these myths in any shape or fashion. The living of an active mysticism – life as metaphor, life as meaningful ritual – are realities that some of us are just beginning to 'plug into' as we seek to expand our consciousness and begin to return to the basic wisdom that has been lost. There is no reason why this wisdom should not include lost knowledge of interstellar visitors.

Monuments on Mars

Speculation about life on our nearest planetary neighbour is hardly new. We now know that life, at least as we know it, cannot exist on the surface of Mars. However, there are those who assert that life could have existed on Mars, in times that are relatively recent by galactic standards, and that the atmosphere on Mars may have been stripped away by some dreadful cataclysm, such as collision with a large meteor. If so, there is a possibility that an ancient Martian civilization left us warnings, encoded in sculptures on the planet's surface.

Pieces of rock are thrown at times from the surface of Mars and land periodically on earth. Two meteorites known to have originated on

Mars are believed by some scientists to contain evidence of extremely primitive microscopic life. These may have existed on Mars as recently as 600,000 years in the past. Some of the tests conducted by the Viking expeditions in 1976 also suggested life. However, the most interesting and controversial evidence, not only for life on Mars, but extremely advanced intelligent life has been provided photographically by the probes Mariner 9 and Viking 1, although this 'evidence' is not regarded as convincing by many experts.

What the pictures seem to show are geometric structures that cannot have originated naturally. Four 'pyramids', much huger than their terrestrial equivalents, appear to have been built in an alignment similar to Giza, in a location on Mars called Elysium. Half-way around Mars, in another area called Cydonia, more pyramids were located. Cydonia is found at a latitude of approximately 40 degrees north. This area, which is similar in size to Greater London, could be seen as a collection of cyclopean ruins. The most notable feature is the 'Face', reminiscent of the Sphinx, and apparently also wearing the headdress of the Egyptian pharaohs.

Some 16km (10 miles) from the Face is a five-sided pyramid, aligned almost perfectly to the north-south Martian axis. Other groupings of structures include four mounds centred on a fifth mound at the exact centre of the 'city' and a large mound echoing Silbury Hill. In addition to Cydonia and Elysium, there are other sites suggestive of intelligent origin, including a row of small pyramids in a straight line 5km (3 miles) long. Photographs taken from different angles indicate that the impressions are unlikely to be illusory.

NASA has dismissed the Face as a trick of the light. However, there have been 'inaccuracies' and questionable statements made in this connection, leading conspiracy theorists to believe the worst. The loss of the Observer probe on its way to Mars in 1993 has been deemed suspicious, because the telemetry with the probe was deliberately shut down. Prior to this, in September 1976, Viking 2 had not landed in Cydonia, because the latitude was too high for radar, and yet Viking eventually landed at an even higher latitude. This decision was taken hot on the heels of discovery of the Face. Probes sent to Mars tend to be ill-fated, and two Russian probes

were lost or destroyed in 1988. The second one, Phobos 2, met its end while photographing one of the Martian moons, its namesake 'Phobos'. One of the last pictures it sent back included an enormous shadow on the surface of Mars, shaped like an cigar, and many kilometres long.

Analyses of photographs of the Face, while not conclusive, point towards the fact that it certainly is a 'face', not a construct of the brain as one may see a face in curtain folds or in a stone wall. However, that in itself does not categorically confirm artificiality. Also interesting to consider are the dimensions of the enormous pyramid, called the D & M Pyramid, situated almost 16km (10 miles) from the Face. This pyramid is pentagonal, and incorporates an ancient sacred proportion called the Golden Section, which was used in many earthly structures (whose significance we are also unsure about). Other geometric and geographical properties also strongly suggest artificiality in Martian structures.

Many claims and counter-claims have been made regarding Cydonia and the Face, and some of the actions of NASA have been regarded as questionable, to say the least. In *The Mars Mystery* Hancock, Bauval and Grigsby point out that under the terms of the Space Act of 1958 NASA has a duty to withhold any information deemed to be a threat to national security. NASA, say the authors, is not a '"Starship Enterprise" on a "mission to seek out new worlds and new civilisations..." On the contrary it is the disturbed child of two dysfunctional parents – paranoia and war.' Indeed, NASA was formed when the Cold War was at its height. Whatever NASA is doing in relation to the Martian monuments and the Face, it is not being straight. For instance, when the first frame from Viking was released in July 1976, showing the Face, officials at press conference claimed that it was just a trick of the light and that another frame taken at a different angle confirmed this. Over 17 years later, officials had to admit that such a picture does not exist. In 1998 the Surveyor probe sent back an image of the controversial visage that appeared to deflate the believers, because it was a mess. However, some pointed out that the image released was the worst one, without the benefit of the usual scientific enhancement, being the least representative of the true landscape and so naturally unlikely

to look like the earlier, Viking pictures. In addition, Hancock and his co-authors tell us:

> *Some pointed out that the Face had been photographed early a.m. on the 5th [April 1998] and yet it waited until 9 a.m. on the 6th to be analysed – lying apparently untouched in the Project databases all night until the start of the next working day, time enough, some might say, for the images to have been altered.*

In *The Mars Mystery* Hancock *et al* expand on the possible significance of the Martian monuments as warnings of a possible cataclysm. As we know, these have visited the earth before, for instance in the case of the K/T meteor that is said to have wiped out the dinosaurs. Our solar system is peppered with giant meteors, comet fragments and the like, any of which could hit us at some point. The K/T object is believed to have been 10 kilometres (6 miles) in diameter, tiny by galactic standards, and yet quite large enough to create a 200-km (125-mile) crater, tidal waves over a kilometre (⅔ mile) high, global wildfires and a following 'nuclear winter' caused by dust and smoke in the atmosphere. Any species not eliminated by the original impact would hardly have survived the freezing cold and utter darkness that followed. Being smaller, a similar impact could have stripped Mars of its atmosphere and its water, thus effectively murdering it, destroying all hope of the resurgence of life. Could the structures on Mars constitute some kind of a warning, by a race that foresaw their fate? If we are advanced enough to decipher the message, we are also sufficiently advanced to avert disaster, theoretically.

Let us therefore end this chapter with some of the warnings issued by the authors of *The Mars Mystery*. Humanity needs to turn its abilities in the direction of preservation, not war, and its imagination towards the possibilities and probabilities approaching us from the far reaches of space, not into better methods of mass destruction. Whatever the message of the ancient astronauts, it seems essentially a moral one. We can survive if we deserve to, and if we 'deserve to' this will be proven by our using our wits constructively. Perhaps we should give a thought to the 'old gods' so we are not taken by surprise.

7

тbe mind's eye

'Tis education forms the common mind,
Just as the twig is bent, the tree's inclined.

Alexander Pope (1688–1744), *Moral Essays*, Epistle 1

dismissing тbe pbenomenon

The term UFO has come to be synonymous with alien craft. However, if
we return to the initial meaning of the acronym, a UFO is an
'Unidentified Flying Object'. During the twentieth century thousands
of rational 'normal' individuals have reported seeing such objects. In
1990 the Belgian government went on record as accepting the fact
that there had been, indeed, unidentifiable craft, believed to be of
unearthly origin, in our skies, after a spate of sightings and radar
tracking. Only the very foolish would deny that something is going on.

If we are determined not to believe in extra-terrestrial intelligent life
forms regularly visiting our planet, what explanations do we have?
Hoax is a favourite with the die-hard non-believer, and indeed there
have been many hoaxes in connection with UFOs. One of the most
impressive of these may have been Majestic 12, discussed in
Chapter 5, although this has not yet been proved conclusively, as far
as I am aware. What might be the motives behind such hoaxes? In
fact there are several. Firstly, they often brighten up lives which can
be dull and uneventful. Secondly, they may lend importance to the

95

person making up the sensational stories. Thirdly, and possibly most importantly, they give a sense of power and superiority to the perpetrator, who may laugh up his or her sleeve at having 'taken in' so many experts. Elaborate hoaxes have been carried out with crop circle manufacture. Hoax may also stem from a deep wish for it to be true, or even a form of ritual acknowledgement of the 'real' phenomenon. However, there have been many sightings that are most unlikely to have been hoaxes, for instance those by high-flying pilots, and it is unclear how a hoax could show up on radar, unless it was the stuff of sci-fi itself (or the radar operators were 'in' in the game).

Among the scientific community there seems to be a great urge to explain any phenomena by 'ordinary' means, even when these are, in effect, more far-fetched than the idea of aliens. For instance, following the Kenneth Arnold initial 'saucer' sighting in 1947 and the ensuing flap, the astronomer Dr Jan Schilt, professor at Columbia University went on record with the explanation that the phenomena were related to similar events in World War II, where speeding aeroplanes disturbed the atmosphere and distorted light rays, and that electricity might also be involved, because of the propellor and wings creating types of smoke rings! It must be remembered that posts for astronomers were, and are, in short supply, and any support for the idea of extra-terrestrials amounts to professional suicide.

Other favourite explanations include theories about mass hypnosis, hysteria, drugs, alcohol, self-deception and 'imagination'. Discounting the idea of chemical interference, which is certainly not relevant in the majority of cases, could this phenomenon be 'all in the mind'? If this were to be the case, the implications for the human race are still important, perhaps as important as the arrival of real extra-terrestrials.

The collective unconscious

The pioneering psychologist and erstwhile disciple of Freud, Carl Gustav Jung introduced the concept of the collective unconscious. We are familiar with the idea of the subconscious or unconscious

mind and many people these days do not find it difficult to accept that there are parts of their minds which are normally inaccessible, but are nonetheless real and have an effect on thought and action. For instance, it is well known that childhood trauma may be 'forgotten' because it is too painful to deal with, or that some fairly mundane event might assume terrifying proportions because of surrounding conditions. The details may be forgotten, but the fear remains. As an example, a two-year-old might come into a quiet room in the house to look for a lost toy. As she goes in, a vase of flowers on the windowsill looms in a rather threatening silhouette, from her tiny perspective. As she is looking at the flowers, trying to make sense of what she sees, older brother bursts from a hiding place under the table, yelping and shrieking. The little girl cries hysterically, and mother confronts her: 'It's only your brother, don't worry, look, it's only him,' etc.' The little girl may have no words to describe her unease at the flower pot, that may now become inextricably linked with terror. This may result in a fear of flowers, or a fear of spiders, for the flowers in outline might have looked like a large spider, or some other fear. Whatever the case, the fear becomes imbedded in the unconscious. The cause cannot be recalled and the only manifestation observable in adult life is the fear, so we may say the fear has unconscious causes. Here we refer to the 'personal unconscious'.

The 'collective unconscious' is, however, common to all of us and is part of our genetic and psychic inheritance as human beings. Buried more deeply than the personal unconscious, collective matters are shared by all of the human race, presumably having their roots in the Stone Ages and before, comprising the entire inner experience of humankind. Because fear of spiders and snakes is very general, some root in the collective may be suspected, perhaps reaching back into a time-before-time when these creatures were larger and more dangerous than they are now, or to some universal symbolism. To understand the concept of the collective unconscious, we might visualize each of us as an island, rising into the light of day from the depths of a deep ocean. The part of our land mass that is revealed by the tides we could equate to the subconscious, those parts of the mind that are accessible if we try but are not readily conscious.

Below this, always under the water but still recognizable as the underpart of the 'island' lies the personal unconscious. Many fathoms below the surface, however, the body of the island connects with the ocean bed and becomes one with the bed-rock of all the other islands. This is the realm of the collective unconscious.

The collective unconscious is therefore the sum of our instinctive humanity, but I interpret it as rather more than a collection of deeply buried impulses and associations. The collective unconscious has relevance to the meaning and purpose of our development as a species and to our spiritual essence. The unconscious speaks to us in archetypal symbols, and these are most discernable in dreams. Thus a modern business person may have dreams that incorporate symbols found painted in caves by Stone Age people. These symbols have the same meaning now as then. A simple example consists of the square, which means earthbound matter, concrete reality, and the circle, which signifies the psyche – thus reconnecting us with the theme of the 'flying saucer'.

Circle and mandala

The mandala is an archetype of the collective unconscious, meaning wholeness. It is a circular design, also comprising elements of the square, thus it echoes the quartered circle used by occultists, meaning the union of matter and mind, the soul finding its roots, the roots reaching up to the sky. Many ancient towns and buildings were constructed with this concept in mind, emphasising the connection between human and cosmos, mind and environment. The ancients, who enjoyed 'participation mystique' did not feel themselves to be separate from their environment but a part of it. The routine of day and night became a drama, as experienced by the human psyche in touch with its feeling responses, and this was translated into myth, such as the eating of the sun-god by the dragon of the West, the sojourn in the belly of the dragon and rebirth next morning. In myth, human nature found a way to express the essential blending of inner and outer. The mandala symbolizes psychic wholeness, craved by modern humans, isolated in our 'objective' minds. It means internal

balance and also connection with the rest of existence, and, lost in our concrete jungles, imprisoned by our own 'logic' knowingly or unknowingly, we crave it.

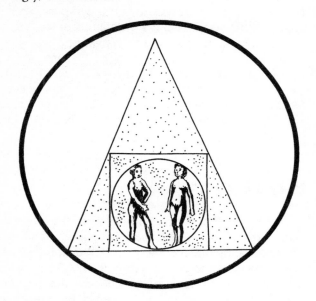

The archetypal image of the mandala, fundamental to reports of UFOs and flying saucers, may link the phenomena with the very depths of the human psyche...

In *Man & His Symbols* (Picador, 1978) Aniela Jaffe has this to say:

> *The symbol of the circle has played a curious part in ... the life of our day .... In the last years of the Second World War, there arose the 'visionary rumour' of round flying bodies that became known as flying saucers or UFOs ... Jung has explained the UFOs as a projection of a psychic content (of wholeness) that has at all times been symbolised by the circle. In other words, this 'visionary rumour', as can also be seen in many dreams of our time, is an attempt by the unconscious collective psyche to heal the split in our apocalyptic age by means of the symbol of the circle.*

Thus we may understand the sightings of flying saucers, arising spontaneously as visions to many people as symbolic of a need for wholeness in these troubled times. They are, therefore, highly significant, but not 'real' in the sense we normally understand the word. This approach has value because it means that we take the phenomenon seriously, as having worth and meaning, and it is also quite comfortable for those who do not want to deal with the inconvenience of 'real' extra-terrestrials. While it is very important to reflect on what these sightings may 'mean' for us, I am not sure that it is the whole story, or that to split 'reality' into inner and outer is the answer. Besides, as a small point, we should note that not all sightings are of circular craft.

The Shadow

Another Jungian concept that surfaces in regard to the entire question of UFOs is that of the Shadow. The Shadow consists of all that we repress within us as being unacceptable, or diabolical. It is what we do not want to be, because to encompass it means we experience a kind of inner 'death'. The contents of the Shadow may be formed from childhood experiences, where we internalized the notion that to be messy/rebellious/stupid/slow meant that we would be a sort of non-person. Sometimes 'good' qualities can also be repressed for the same reasons, as in 'no-one in our family puts on airs and graces'. The child recipient of that piece of dogma may consign refinement and good manners to the Shadow. The Shadow is what we hate about ourselves, what we can never allow ourselves to be in a month of Sundays. It stands at the threshold of the unconscious and, until we make efforts to own and incorporate it, we can never really begin to know ourselves. However, owning the Shadow may be a matter of excruciating shame and self-hatred, at least at first. Many people 'project' their Shadow, seeing it embodied in others and hating them, saying 'I could never be like that' when in fact a part of us is very much 'like that'. This doesn't mean, of course, that certain things aren't indeed hateful, but is rather a matter of spotting

a self-righteous tone, a slight lack of balance in the viewpoint. The Shadow can be spotted anywhere where someone is declaring their 'pet hates' and a parlour game destined to break up any party is 'Shadow-spotting' – defining the repressed parts of the personality on the basis of what each person hates!

The personal Shadow might manifest itself in 'I really hate scruffy people, or salesman-types or people who just sit and say nothing', which may mean there is an internal tramp, a Mr Slick or a Miss Mouse dying to get out. However, collective Shadows are much more dangerous. These may surface as racial or religious hatred. The most noxious example was that of the Nazis – the blond Aryan race whose Shadow fell upon the Jews, resulting in the Holocaust.

So how might this connect with our subject of UFOs? I think we may discern it in conspiracy theories, where all manner of reprehensible goings-on are attributed to a government in league with aliens, coldly exploiting unwitting humans in their ghastly experiments. This does not, of course, mean that there are no conspiracies, cover-ups or the like, but that the whole thing acquires more voltage and a lot less reasoned thought because it plugs in to so many psychological factors. Where there is a lack of understanding, of communication and of openness, such psychological weeds can flourish. The entire climate of UFO research is one that encourages psychological imbalance, inviting unconscious elements to rampage. This needs to be born in mind by the serious researcher.

Shamanism

Shamanism is essentially the art of spirit flight, believed to have been practised almost universally in prehistoric times. The shaman would enter a trance, going into the world of the spirits, gods and demons, in order to obtain relevant information or wisdom to impart to the tribe. Here we see a faith in a 'reality' not immediately apparent to the physical senses and the idea that meaningful information can be drawn forth from abstract realms. More than this, by acting in these

abstract realms, real change can be wrought in this world. This is a practice that is being revitalized by present-day shamans in healing techniques.

Jung, who made so many ancient beliefs and models relevant in a modern, psychological context, saw UFOs as a 'visionary rumour'. In our time, religion has been reduced to dogma and sets of rules, with true spiritual revelation regarded with suspicion. The material world and the physical world have been split asunder, with beliefs about the former tightly policed, on the one hand by proponents of the monotheistic faiths who have only one source of revelation, and on the other by rationalists, who will just about tolerate 'belief in God' and such like, as long as it makes no incursion into daily life. In such a climate the visionary may become secularized, with ordinary people, even the technologically clued up and highly-trained, such as fighter pilots, becoming channels for an alternative vision, an idea of 'wholeness' and a possible message for the human race that we are at an evolutionary crossroads.

Promoters of the Ancient Astronaut Theory, notably Erich von Daniken, linked many ancient relics and artefacts with beings from another world (see Chapter 6). Notably, the straight lines on the Nazca pampa in South America were believed to be the 'runways' for extra-terrestrial craft, bringing visitors from the stars to prehistoric humanity, along with undreamed-of technological skill, that was used in the construction of the pyramids and similar. A modern theory for these lines holds that they are an externalization of inner reality, the spirit flight of the shaman, which usually (although not always) takes place in a straight line. This is an interesting linkage of ideas, for either way UFOs feature as a type of emissary, an inward one to the modern (or ancient) shamen, or an outer one, bringing 'real' beings with their attendant gifts of advancement. The lines on the Nazca pampa link with the straight line formations that have been observed in the British Isles, known as 'ley lines'. Some people believe that these lines are energy lines, channels upon the surface of the earth, and UFO sightings have been seen to cluster around them.

Currently, some Native American shamans now report contact with extra-terrestrials, who bring an awesome message about the future and the responsibilities of humanity. In the developed world, UFO

visionaries abound and we have already encountered some of these for instance in George King, founder of the Aetherius Society. Channelled messages from enlightened extra-terrestrials are very common. In a way this is a new 'religion' bringing messages of peace, enlightenment and global brother and sisterhood. We may see the concept of the extra-terrestrial as being the modern version of the angel, simply the form with which these revelations clothe themselves on their passage through the human psyche. This does not render the message any less significant, but it does, naturally, have a bearing on whether we regard aliens as objectively real or not.

The nature of reality

At the root of most UFO research lies the wish to prove that they are 'real' (or not real), not to find out what they mean for us in terms of the evolution of our concepts. However, only because we so relentlessly split inner and outer reality are these two quests so apparently divided. To traditional peoples, such as the Native Americans, all that we do is a metaphor for spirit, daily life is, itself, symbolic. To those of us grounded in everyday reality this can be a difficult concept, but to more so-called 'primitive' people this world and Otherworld intertwine. One rather inadequate example of this can be found in modern times, in astrology, which turns symbols into everyday life, draws deep significance from the passage of the planets, etc. Thus Mars is not simply a small, red planet but the significator of possible war, a manifestation of the 'war god', etc. As the three extra-Saturnian planets were discovered, so the elements they govern in life came to the fore. For instance, Uranus, planet of rebellion, was discovered at the time of the French Revolution, Neptune, planet of the insubstantial, of dreams, ideals, and visions, was discovered as anaesthetics came into use and mesmerism and spiritualism became popular, while the discovery of Pluto, planet of profound change, coincided with the atom bomb. This is a very restricted example of a totally different mind set from that of the Western mind, where all is interconnected in a web of beingness.

However, we all know that we can't influence practical matters just by thinking about them. Or so says received wisdom. We are observers of reality, we cannot change it, except on its own terms. We do not create reality, we only influence it by practical intervention. But what if this were not true? What if reality, far from being something in which we participate, sometimes reluctantly, were to be something we actually create? This sounds like the stuff of pure fantasy, but in fact brushes on ideas of relativity. In fact, it has been proved that an observer *does* effect the process of an experiment, merely by being there.

An example provided by quantum physics demonstrates this. A beam of light which is shone through a tiny hole will cause a small circle of light to appear on an appropriately positioned screen. Two tiny holes made side by side will result in two overlapping circles of light, but where they intersect there will occur some dark lines, because the two beams interfere with each other, partially cancelling each other out. Light 'particles' are called 'photons'. If the beams are now reduced so that each stream consists of a single photon at a time, the interference lines ought, by rights, to disappear, as a single photon cannot interfere with another. However, the lines are still there. Yet, if the photons are watched with a photon detector to see what is going on, the pattern of interference disappears. It is at this quantum level that science is beginning to detect the very real influence that mind has upon matter. Further than this, physics also teaches us that matter is, in fact, energy, and that what we see as solid objects may be a kind of localized disturbance in the energy field.

So terms such as 'reality', 'mind' and 'matter' are in the melting pot as the old millennium gives way to the new. There are those who feel that we are on the verge of a breakthrough in consciousness, where we will become conscious of other dimensions and those who inhabit them, and this is the opinion of many writers and seers, old and new. I cannot phrase it better than in a passage from my recent publication *The Millennium and Beyond* (Hodder, 1998):

> *Are we ready to make some breakthrough in our evolution, into a fresh comprehension of the Universe? It is hard to imagine the existence of other dimensions and we can readily do this only by analogy. Imagine a two-dimensional world of Flatland, where the*

*inhabitants were aware only of length and breadth; for them
height had no existence. And then imagine a three-dimensional
being like ourselves interacting with them and attempting to
communicate. This would be extremely difficult for we would
have no frames of reference for our three-dimensional
consciousness in their terminology. Our manifestations would
seem miraculous and probably haphazard and most mysterious –
just like the alien phenomena ... suppose that some of our 'aliens'
are, in fact, consciousnesses from a further dimension...*

This idea was the basis for the sinister television series *Invasion
Earth*, broadcast in 1998, where beings from another dimension
invaded earth, to turn it over into a vast farm, for their own use.
However, it is more pleasant to think that something more productive
is at work. In *Alien Impact* (see Further reading) Michael Craft quotes
the words of researcher Jacques Vallée: 'If the phenomenon is forcing
us through a learning curve *it has no choice but to mislead us*'. Craft
likens us, tellingly but unappealingly, to rats in a maze, conditioned
by cycles that are regular yet unpredictable. Unpleasant stimulus
encourages us to undertake new behaviour. What that behaviour
may be or should be, is unclear. Possibly we are being reconditioned
by alien beings or by our higher selves, or even more strangely,
perhaps these are more or less the same thing. It is hard to imagine
what the next step in our evolution may be, because if we can
'imagine' it then we are, essentially, already 'there'.

Maybe a new 'consciousness' could encompass a fresh perspective
on time, which is the next 'dimension' through which we move while
having no control of our destiny. Possibly we shall develop a global
awareness that extends beyond humanitarian behaviour into a true
and conscious participation in creation. At a very basic level the
Star Trek film *First Contact* depicts how a meeting with extra-
terrestrials did indeed unite the human race in a new vision of itself,
where its internal squabbles seemed no longer relevant.

Whatever the actualities, and they may be many and more than
even the wildest ufologist can imagine, it is likely that UFOs fulfil a
need. Not a need for the sensational, although that is part of the
scene, but the need for a catalyst, something to bring about a

change in our viewpoint. Our current 'viewpoint' may be seen as extremely destructive, with no immediate solution in sight, certainly not from conventional sources. Whatever the 'message' of the UFOs, perhaps we should approach them not as believers, but with open minds, eager for education. We need it.

PRACTICE

If you would like to obtain a fuller understanding of the works and concepts of Jung, an excellent book to start with is An *Introduction to Jung's Psychology* by Frieda Fordham (Penguin, 1985).

You may also like to reflect on the nature of 'reality' and what the experience of UFOs may be indicating to us concerning this. Do not be afraid to entertain 'outlandish' notions, because you have been told they are not reasonable. The poet, painter and visionary William Blake referred to 'Jesus, the imagination'. In our imaginations we may find a teacher and a saviour.

fURTHER READING

The Roswell File Tim Shawcross, Bloomsbury, 1997. A valuable, thorough and unbiased investigation of Roswell.

The Roswell Incident Charles Berlitz & William Moore, Granada, 1980. A readable account of Roswell.

Both the above titles yielded information for the chapter on the Roswell incident, and are a good starting point for further research.

The Philadelphia Experiment Terry Deary, Kingfisher, 1996. A fictionalized story of the Philadelphia Experiment.

The Philadelphia Experiment: Project Invisibility Charles Berlitz & William Moore, Souvenir, 1979. In-depth look at the 'experiment'.

Both the above works have been useful for the chapter on the Philadelphia Experiment.

The Mars Mystery Hancock, Bauval & Grigsby, Penguin, 1998 A fascinating and detailed account of the monuments on Mars and the relevance of Mars and its fate in respect of our own future.

UFOs & Ufology: The First 50 Years Paul Devereux & Peter Brookesmith, Blandford, 1998. Up-to-date, comprehensive and attractively presented, with lots of visual material.

Alien Impact Michael Craft, St Martin's, 1996. Compelling reading and highly comprehensive coverage of the alien phenomenon. Recommended.

The Sirius Mystery Robert Temple, Arrow, 1999. Fascinating evidence of alien contact 5,000 years in the past. Important reading.

Other Works and Resources

The UFO Encyclopedia Margaret Sachs, Corgi, 1981
Mysteries Colin Wilson, Grafton, 1986
From Atlantis To The Sphinx Colin Wilson, Virgin, 1997
Sightings Susan Michaels, Fireside, 1996
The Millennium & Beyond Teresa Moorey, Hodder & Stoughton, 1999
The Twelfth Planet Zachariah Sitchin, Avon, 1976
Chariots Of The Gods? Erich von Daniken, Putnam, 1970
Gold Of The Gods Erich von Daniken, Souvenir Press, 1973
The Complete Books Of Charles Fort Charles Fort, Dover, 1974
Communion Whitley Strieber, Avon, 1987
Man & His Symbols edited by C.G. Jung, Picador, 1978
Flying Saucers: A Modern Myth Of Things Seen In The Sky Princeton
  University Press, 1978
The Montauk Project Preston Nichols, Sky Books, 1992
Nothing in this Book is True, But it's Exactly How Things Are
  Bob Frisell, Frog Ltd, 1994
The Monuments of Mars Richard Hoagland, North Atlantic Press, 1995

The Circular Forum
Gloucestershire's UFO Groups, President Robin Cole. 12 Dagmar
Road Tivoli, Cheltenham Glos GL50 2UG Tel: 01242 577629
Major International Conference to be held in association with *UFO*
magazine, at Cheltenham Town Hall, Feb 18–20th 2000. Facilities
for 100 guests. Contact Robin Cole for more information. Robin is
the author of *GCHQ & the UFO Cover Up* from which I have quoted.

Fortean Times magazine available from bookstands, or phone
01454 202515 (outside UK +441454 202515).

Amateur Astronomy & Earth Sciences available from bookstands
tel 01223 502196 (UK +44).